SAVING FIVE

AUWA BOOKS

MCD / FARRAR, STRAUS AND GIROUX

NEW YORK

SAVING FIVE

A Memoir of Hope

AMANDA NGUYEN

AUWA Books
MCD / Farrar, Straus and Giroux
120 Broadway, New York 10271

Library of Congress Control Number: 2024035147
ISBN: 978-0-374-61591-8

Designed by Gretchen Achilles

Our books may be purchased in bulk for promotional,
educational, or business use. Please contact your local bookseller
or the Macmillan Corporate and Premium Sales Department at
1-800-221-7945, extension 5442, or by email at
MacmillanSpecialMarkets@macmillan.com.

www.auwabooks.com • www.mcdbooks.com • www.fsgbooks.com
Follow us on social media at @mcdbooks

1 3 5 7 9 10 8 6 4 2

The names and identifying characteristics of some persons
described in this book have been changed.

This book is written for every survivor.
May these pages help you heal. May they help
you find hope. May they help to show you
that you will make it through.

CONTENTS

CONTENTS

SAVING FIVE

1.

Finding Her

I go back to the place I was raped. It's been ten years—a decade of life, and a world away from the person I was then. And yet, I feel her. Her pain. Her loneliness. Her despair. Her powerful rage.

Scientific studies on memory explain the peculiar impact that trauma can have on the brain. Out there in the world, your body is attacked—and inside your head, a hormone called norepinephrine is released, spawning an emotionally charged reaction: the violent birth of a memory. For years, perhaps, or even for the rest of your life, your brain can keep that memory loaded in the chamber, slick with adrenaline, ready to fire away with the tug of a trigger.

The building where the attack occurred is a regular

building. Bricks. A dorm room. I walk up to it, my shoes clacking against the stone path. There she is, still sitting on the steps. Me at 22.

"Why have you come back? Don't you remember what they did to me? To *us*?" she hisses at me, a synapse burning electric in the back of my head.

Her pain roots me to the ground. My body tingles, feeling her despair. I let her speak.

"Well, did you get justice for us?" she shrieks, tears pouring out of her eyes. Her voice changes to a whisper, as if afraid to know the answer. "Did we win?"

"We did." I smile gently at her.

Deep breath.

"But it cost everything," I admit. "Our youth, our relationships, our dreams."

"Was it worth it?" she asks.

A pause. A bracing wind blows. Gentle rain has started to fall.

"Yes. Every second of it. A life worth living is one that is free."

I feel my chest tighten. A truth pours out.

"You exist in a place of extraordinary pain," I tell her. "We were outraged when it started—we wanted to burn the world, and we were ready to burn with it. The first law we passed carried the voice of a bloodcurdling scream. But with each law—and each moment—that passes, that voice has changed. It carries a song today: a chorus of justice.

"In moments of stress, wherever you are, close your eyes. If you listen really hard, the wind carries a song for you.

4

"The wind blows.

"Do you hear it? It is the steady beat of thousands of footsteps for centuries to come. A path, a new reality already made possible because you existed. The choir is already singing."

We hold on to each other. Hand in hand we take the first step, walking to the tunnel where the dorm exit gates are. Our steps echo in unison. The iron hinges creak as I pull on the gate. She stops me before we leave.

"There were happy memories here, too. Friends who loved us. Who still love you," 22 says.

The memory of our laughter echoes in the tunnel.

"The worst thing that happened to us doesn't have to define this place. You can take it back. You get to decide what this place, and these people, will mean," 22 continues.

"Thank you," I tell her.

I raise my hand to wipe the tears from my face. As I do, I realize she's not holding on anymore. She is gone, at peace, satisfied with my answer.

Deep breath. I close my eyes. It is over.

I walk past the gate and down the stone steps. The breeze rustles the leaves. I smell the rain-kissed land. I hear birds chirping. There are no predators here anymore.

I look up at the sky. Raindrops join the tears of release across my face. The choir sings in the wind.

2.

RABBIT

Harvard, 2013

Fuck, everything hurts. Something is wrong. Really, really wrong.

People commonly learn about two responses to danger: fight or flight. We're not taught that there's a third: freeze. Evolutionary scientists say it's common in prey, as a last desperate measure, to play dead.

My insides feel like liquid magma while simultaneously feeling like cold meat. Like a fucking carcass. How did he get inside me so quickly? Everything happened so fast. With precision. Like it was planned. Like this wasn't his first time. Like he'd done it before. I feel like vomiting. Heavy nausea descends. My body is shutting down. Immobile. I have to get help.

The instinct of fight, flight, or freeze has been ingrained

in humankind from our earliest days—it is lodged so deeply in our brains that we couldn't shut it off if we tried. Our nervous system courses chemicals through our bodies: in this case, a red alert. Some of us run, like a gazelle from a lion. Some of us fight, like red and black ants. Some of us stay still—a simulation of death—like a rabbit when it knows a wolf is near. I suppose I'm like a rabbit.

I like rabbits. They're one of my favorite animals. But I would never say it's the rabbit's fault when it's eaten. Rabbits weren't born to be eaten. They're cute and lovely—if a wolf eats one, I would say fuck that wolf.

How could my body betray me like this?

There is a voice inside me that screams, *Get help.*

Charlize. Charlize would know what to do. Fuck. Fuck. Fuck.

A stifling blanket of guilt falls over me.

I should have gone to her stupid protest instead of the party. I should have listened to Charlize.

Get help. Text Charlize. There's that voice again.

She's going to judge me. I'm a hypocrite for not going to the protest—a call to support the very type of person I've just become. A survivor.

Who the fuck cares. Get help now. Go to the hospital now. If Charlize is who she says she is, she'll help you.

I'm crawling on the floor of my dorm room, fighting my neurological response, fighting against millennia of conditioned evolutionary instinct to drag my body to my lifeline: my phone. The bruised lower half of my body is completely numb. I use my forearms to carry my weight.

My fingers fumble to grasp and unlock my phone. I open iMessage and click on her name: Charlize.

The cursor blinks.

. . .

There is more than one way to die. Kill spirits. Kill hope. Kill time.

I've just died. The type of death where you're left behind to endure being alive on the outside—no matter how dead you now feel inside. That's what rape can do.

My death took place at Harvard. Harvard was supposed to be my dream—but today it has become my nightmare. Today will forever be the day that I was raped. The death of my inner life. The worst thing that will ever happen to me.

Until something else happens—a second betrayal.

All good stories have great villains. The best villains are reasonable, in their own way. You understand their point of view. Sometimes they are even cool; sometimes they have rhythm.

I know what my villain sounds like. She takes on many appearances. Smooth sand slipping through an hourglass. The click of a stopwatch. The resounding second hand of a clock.

Tick.

Time is the great equalizer. Brutal fairness, sliced into equal pieces.

Tick.

Time spares no one. All gods bow down before it, even death. But there is one thing that wins over time.

Tick.

Justice. Justice is so powerful she bends the moral arc of the universe.

Tick.

When justice arrives, time runs out.

Tick.

If you do not find justice in this life, make it. If the rules are shit, rewrite them.

Tick.

This is the story of how I penned my own civil rights into existence. This is the story of how I beat time.

Tick.

9 HOURS UNTIL THE RAPE

Before I became known for the worst day of my life, I was a student, like any other student, trying to find her way through life.

Tick. I watch the second hand of a clock that sits above the chalkboard. Eleven fifty-nine a.m.

It's a big lecture hall. About two hundred students. I'm seated near the door, my laptop already packed in a brown leather slingback.

"Class dismissed," my government professor proclaims.

A rush of students slams shut their laptops and notebooks. I'm the first one out, dashing down the wooden stairs, past a corkboard full of bright red flyers, and out to my bike. A cute red-and-white beach cruiser with a wire basket and a silver bell leans next to an oak tree drooping with red and orange autumn leaves. I unhook the bike lock and throw it into the basket. When the basket isn't filled with books, I like to fill it with flowers. Sunflowers used to be my favorite since they look so cheery, but ever since I moved to snowy Cambridge, I've started liking tulips. The gardeners on campus plant them every fall, and they fully bloom in the spring. It reminds me that life exists after winter.

Most times I tie my hair up in a crimson velvet ribbon before I ride, but today I don't have the time. The breeze lifts my long, black hair as the bike glides to a constant velocity. I don't want to be late to office hours with my favorite professor, Dimitar Sasselov, a leading scholar of exoplanets, which are planets outside our solar system. If you discover a planet in class, you get an automatic A. I did not discover one when I took his first class—and although I did get an A, I still plan to discover one once I get out of school and embark on my career. How cool would that be?! Plus, rumor has it that you can name your planet if you discover it. I'd name mine Lucky, after my beloved first dog, a golden retriever that wandered into my childhood home when I was five.

Dimitar's office is in the Harvard–Smithsonian Center for Astrophysics. When you step inside, you're greeted by gorgeous globes of our solar system's planets. Details of Mars's canyons, Jupiter's big red eye, Saturn's rings. Star charts as far as the eye can see. People walk through here like they are on the verge of a discovery that will change the course of history and our understanding of the universe. And it's true. You feel like anything and everything is possible in this building. Because it is. It's my happy place on campus.

It takes ten minutes to bike from gov to the astrophysics department, but if I go quickly I can do it in under seven, which is the grace period for being late. I pedal down Mount Auburn Street, passing by Alpha Phi, where my sorority sisters are planning tonight's hangout with the men's final club. It's October, my birthday month. In fact, it's my birthday week. Three days ago I turned twenty-two years old. My Alpha Phi sisters had planned a birthday dinner for me at a local Thai restaurant. This is my last semester in college. In three months I'll graduate and head to Washington, DC. I'll miss my girlfriends so much, but I'm also so excited to pursue my dreams in the nation's capital—*"Where all roads lead if you want to change the world!"* my gov professor tells us. And I do want to change the world—or simply discover worlds unknown. I just don't know which path to take yet.

What I do know is that the only place that makes me feel even happier than Harvard's astrophysics department is NASA Headquarters. NASA HQ is in DC, and when I first worked there, it was by mistake. I was only eighteen when I saw the application for their internship. In a place that took college graduates and postdocs as interns, I knew that my age would be a disadvantage. So when I applied, I omitted my graduation year. Everything else was accurate, I just— ahem—*forgot* to put the date I would graduate by. What was the worst that could happen? I'd get rejected? Then I'd be back where I started, and I wouldn't have lost anything. I would, however, have something very serious and real to lose if I didn't try. I applied to dozens of summer opportunities that year—scholarships, jobs, internships. They were about more than career advancement for me. They were an escape from what had come before, what was still waiting for me. They were a way to stay safe, so that I never had to go back to the place I ran away from.

I got the NASA internship at eighteen. It wasn't until two months into the job that my boss realized I was only a sophomore. By then it was too late—we were past the point of liftoff. I loved the NASA team, and they loved me.

8 HOURS UNTIL THE RAPE

I throw my bike into the grass and beep into the astrophysics department with my ID card.

No time to lock it—hopefully no one steals the bike. The elevator is too slow. Stairs it is.

This building has newer, concrete stairs. Dimitar's office is on the third floor. Which is not that many flights, but when you're lugging textbooks that feel like rocks, they can make you question your fitness. I run past the corner of globes. No time to admire them today.

"HELLO, PROFESSOR!" I am full-on panting.

"Amanda! You are always on the go. Don't worry, have some water." Dimitar smiles as he hands me a glass, almost as if he knew I'd be out of breath upon arrival.

His large office faces south. Warm light cascades into the room. The sun's neutrinos spin many radiometers inside. To the right, covering half of his wall, hangs an extra-large eight-by-ten-foot poster of the Kepler exoplanet mission. It features the sections of the night sky that Kepler, a space telescope launched by NASA to discover Earth-size planets, looked at. Kepler is Dimitar's mission. The telescope detected thousands of confirmed planets. That's a lot of A's.

Dimitar is also the director of Harvard's Origins of Life Initiative. That's right—aliens. The fact that his job is to push the boundaries of knowledge and how we understand our place in the universe gives him a constant orbital perspective. It makes him open to new possibilities, which in turn makes him more empathetic. Ironically, the guy who spends his time with his head in the stars is the most grounded human I know. This is our weekly check-in for my senior paper, but we talk as much about my future as we do about our research. That's what I really like about him—he genuinely cares about his students.

Dimitar asks, "So, do you want to work at NASA after graduation? What did Ellen say?"

Ellen Baker. When I say NASA was my family, I mean NASA was my *family*. Christmas is always the hardest time of year for me. When I had nowhere else to go, Ellen and her daughter Meredith, who is my year at Harvard, offered for me to stay with them for Christmas break.

Ellen became an astronaut in 1985. To put that in perspective, Sally Ride had become the first American woman to fly in space just two years before. Prior to Ellen's selection as an astronaut, she graduated from the Air Force Aerospace Medicine course. She flew three times, logging over 686 hours in space. The first picture of Ellen on Google is her in a backward cap, floating in the International Space Station.

Ellen is a straight shooter. Blunt. She's cool in the sense that your incompetence is an affront to her coolness. When her nephew was three hours late for Christmas dinner, she stood outside her home, arms crossed, feet tapping in sync with the passing seconds in military precision. "I would have circled the earth twice by now," she told him when he finally arrived.

I did want to work at NASA. Becoming an astronaut was my dream. But unbeknownst to Dimitar or Ellen, I had started the application process last summer for another government program: the Clandestine Service at the Central Intelligence Agency.

When a CIA recruiter invited me to come meet with him in Virginia last year, he asked me what I thought I was being recruited for.

"Directorate of Intelligence?" I guessed, since I studied national security and astrophysics.

"No." The recruiter chuckled. "Directorate of Operations. Much better fit for you. You know how to survive."

Even though I knew being a spy wasn't my dream, I still went along with the program, content with stretching out and punting the decision for as long as I could instead of having to face the impossible feeling of making a clear-cut choice on my future.

7 HOURS UNTIL THE RAPE

I'm biking back to my dorm now, relieved that no one has stolen my bike. A traffic light halts my glide. Charlize is there on the corner holding a bunch of flyers in her hands, the same red ones tacked in the halls of the gov department. Charlize has short black hair that swoops over to one side. She doesn't have tattoos or piercings, but the very sight of Charlize instills fear in trolls. She is "smash the patriarchy" personified. Her major is, unsurprisingly, in gender and sexuality studies.

Charlize is the founder of Our Harvard Can Do Better and a board member of Know Your IX, two clubs that protest college campus sexual assault. Last semester she carried around a mattress at Harvard as an art performance piece, standing in solidarity with Emma Sulkowicz's protest at Columbia University. I wonder what her latest demonstration will be. I don't have to wait for long. She's about to tell me.

"Amanda! We're meeting up tonight to talk about our next protest. You should come. We'll need everyone. We're thinking of taping red tape to our graduation caps that spells out IX."

Her hand shoots out and plops the flyer into my bike's basket.

"Oh! Um . . . good to see you, Charlize . . . I've got . . . I've unfortunately got a thing then," I mumble.

The light turns green.

Thank god, I think. Between picking out my outfit for the party tonight or planning a protest—which could potentially count against me in my career—I'm going to the party. I think about what Ellen says about the minuscule chances of getting into NASA, especially as a woman. I can't risk getting involved in anything that could jeopardize it.

16

3 HOURS UNTIL THE RAPE

I'm sitting in my dorm, leaning over the sink with a counter of makeup. Lana Del Rey is crooning "Born to Die" on my phone. The heat from the curling iron steams off my hair. My roommate is also in Alpha Phi. We're singing, laughing, and dancing.

"Do you know what you're going to wear to the party?" she asks. This is a question that I'll hear over and over again in my head in the weeks and years to come.

1 HOUR UNTIL THE RAPE

We arrive at the frat. It's a mansion in the middle of campus. This is the last hour before my life is redefined. In this next hour, I'll meet him. He'll describe me as his sister to his final club brothers. We'll laugh about it. It's like he knows something that I don't.

It's like he already planned to rape me that night.

3.

Into the Dark

"There are only two people you need to make proud in your life. Five-year-old you and eighty-year-old you."

"When you change the world, write it all down." That was what people told me. So here I am, running away to find my mind or perhaps to lose it. A sanctuary to quell my thoughts, quiet enough to listen to the drumbeat of my heart. To let my pain breathe. A safe haven to lose my sanity. A mental manifestation of my memory. A place I go within myself. My interior world.

The pen in my hand ignites into a torch for this journey into the abyss of my memory, flickering at the edges of darkness. With every step I take, the past echoes. My stomach churns knowing what I must do: find, confront, and translate the whispers of my ghosts.

Suddenly there she is. Through the haze she arrives, the

facsimile of my yesteryear. At 5 years old, at 15 years old, at 22 years old. We sit together.

"Welcome back, 30."

I look up at the kind voice—it's me at 15, with a crimson velvet ribbon holding half her hair up. The other half is down her back, but not quite at her hips yet, like mine is now. 15 is wearing a preppy sweater and a matching white tennis skirt. She's on the high school tennis team, and even if it's not a prep school, she's dressed like it is. Straight posture, prim and proper, 15 is on her best behavior at all times, nervous to be anything but perfect. The image of a flawless trophy daughter. She's a straight-A student with Harvard in her sights.

"You look . . . different than what I expected."

The voice is coming from someone else now. "I thought you'd be bitchier."

Black leather jacket and black skinny jeans. Her hair is held taut in a high ponytail. She swears a lot—she's disenchanted, pessimistic, and angry. This is the activist version of me at twenty-two, after the rape but before I change the world. She's a protector, jaded and hurt. I don't reply to her comment.

She pauses and circles around me. "Wow, 30, you look like you have money. Lash extensions, nails done, designer clothes. Are you healed yet? Less of my edge, huh . . . Still on edge, though."

"You're judgy," I tell her.

"I'm you," 22 shoots back.

"Okay, okay," 5 says with both palms up, the peacekeeper. 5's hair is braided into two pigtails that extend to the length of her shoulders. She's in jean overalls with brass buttons and little embroidered yellow sunflowers on the top pocket. I study her chubby cheeks, her hopeful, innocent smile.

"5! Your hands!" 15 exclaims.

Sickly, dark purple veins creep from 5's fingertips, climbing up her wrists. She looks inquisitively and calmly turns her palms around. It appears like poison.

"Does it hurt?" I ask.

"Kind of. But I'm sure with rest I'll be fine. I want to hear all our stories," says 5.

"No, we need to find help, 5," 22 demands restlessly.

"It's the right thing to do," 15 agrees. "Right? 30?"

"Right," I declare. "We cannot just sit here and wait in the darkness."

"And besides," says 22, "we need answers."

"Answers?" I respond, unsure of my footing.

"Do our dreams come true?" asks 5.

"Do we make it out?" asks 15.

"Do we survive?" asks 22.

"Well, yes," I tell them, "but it was ugly. And hard, and painful."

5 looks up with a wonder only innocence can radiate. "Tell us."

She embraces my hand in hers. When I unfurl our intertwined fingers, they have transformed into something beautiful, weathered, earned. I look up from our palms into the face of my future, eighty years graceful. With the compassion only time can grant, she says again, "Tell us."

I swing the torch into the darkness of the cave, moving deeper into the uncharted land of our memory. On our way to find help—to find answers.

4.

THE HOSPITAL

The first seventy-two hours after a rape are critical. That's because the crime scene is your body—and like all things biological, your body decays.

"We have to get you in, or else the evidence will be naturally flushed away. At least it hasn't been that long," Charlize says.

It's 1:00 a.m. We're in an Uber on the way to the Brigham and Women's Hospital. I'm hunched over in a fetal position in the back seat. Charlize is sitting next to me. The car bounces over the streets of Cambridge.

We're silent for most of the ride. It feels like a daze. I am half awake in a real-life nightmare.

We're here now. In a big red sign above the door, white letters in all caps spell out EMERGENCY. The sliding doors open. My feet carry me automatically, tracking Charlize's footsteps. My stomach drops; I have no idea what I'm going to say. How do I even begin to describe what I need help for?

Without wasting a beat, Charlize goes up to the front desk.

In matter-of-fact language, Charlize says, "We're here for a rape kit. For my friend." The receptionist nods in understanding.

A *what?* I think. I don't know what a rape kit even is. No matter how humiliated I feel, I'm glad Charlize is here. She knows what to do.

A nurse comes out and brings me in immediately. This is the handover. I turn around and watch as Charlize grows smaller and smaller until the doors of the patient unit close. The only person I know here is gone. I am on my own.

The next six hours define my life.

● ● ●

Pastel green curtains surround the gurney I am on. Bright fluorescent lights buzz above. The gentle beep of a heart monitor tells me I'm alive, no matter how dead I feel inside.

A man in a white coat steps in. He's in his early thirties. He extends his hand, and in as gentle of a voice as he can muster, he says, "I'm Dr. Obermeyer, but you can call me Ziad. I'm sorry you're here under these circumstances today."

I nod, not sure how to respond.

"I went to Harvard too. Dunster House," he says.

"The box that Mather came in," I joked.

We smile briefly before the context of my visit returns. In a moment when I feel utterly alone, the brief recognition of humanity from this doctor, from this stranger, is something that stays with me. I am grasping for kindness.

•   •   •

The plastic hospital band reads:

```
10/10/1991–22F
Service Date: 10/14/13
NGUYEN, AMANDA
```

A woman joins us. She's in scrubs.

"I'm a SANE nurse," she gently explains. "Sexual Assault Nurse Examiner." She takes out a seemingly endless fleet of bottles and cotton swabs.

Another nurse in a ponytail and colorful scrubs wheels a tray over to my bedside. She dumps out about thirty pills on top of it.

"I know it looks like a lot, but I promise it's all to help you," the second nurse says.

"Do you know if you want to press charges?" she asks. "It's not something you have to decide right now. There is a fifteen-year statute of limitations—fifteen years for you to decide. But it will determine whether your name will be attached to this kit."

I try to wrap my head around this information.

"Will I have to go forward with the trial without my consent if I report? Is there a way for me to report without losing agency?"

"That's not for me to determine, but remember the trial is Massachusetts versus the perpetrator. Not you versus the perpetrator."

I learn in this moment that it will never be me versus my rapist. If my assault amounts to anything at all, it will be the government versus my rapist—as if he had committed a crime against the Commonwealth. Am I erased so easily?

We know the names of the men: Bill Cosby, Jeffrey Epstein, R. Kelly. But how many of the women they hurt can we name? In America's criminal justice system, survivors become background characters to a story that is actually about us—our lives, our bodies, our dignity. The battleground for violence against women's bodies can't even pass the Bechdel test. That's just how the system works. Victims are erased from their own narratives. And now I will become, at best, a mere witness to my own rape trial.

I think about my dreams. NASA and the CIA would absolutely demerit a candidate based on whether or not they have an active court case. Both places make you fill out forms to report it. On the precipice of achieving my dreams, while lying in a hospital bed, I am being forced to make a choice: career versus justice.

•   •   •

BWH S/A CHECKLIST AND QUALITY ASSURANCE FORM

Date of Visit

Kit Number

Age

Known/Unk Assailant?

SANE or BWH, RN

Plan B offered?

Reported (Y/N)

SANE Protocol INSTRUCTIONS

Need kit? <120 hrs or <24 hrs if only anal/oral assault

Med clear pt before paging SANE

Pge SANE-Q10min × 2—then BWH protocol

S/A Cart in room with kit. Check/replace expired tubes. The RN who opens kit stays with it until completed

Tox kit, <72 hr of assault (re-fridge ASAP to preserve) Check tox kit for expired tubes.

Complete form 1—consent

If tox kit, obtain separate consent—yellow copy goes inside tox kit

Uhcg/utox (60 cc for tox) 1st/2nd urine has highest drug levels. Instruct not to wipe if applicable

Kit number on all forms/envelopes/nsg & d/c forms

Form 2—info pertaining to assault (same as crime report)

Form 3—pt's "primary hx of events"

Forms 4&5 (completed by MD/PA/SANE)

Check results of hcg & document

ID Consult Mandatory if post exposure prophylactic. Needlestick bb 13690. F/U apt given? If not, why

MD use template in computer to order meds. New Mass Law (MGLc. 111) to offer Plan B

Document and Give HIV/STD/preg PEP (HIV PEP if <72 hrs; 28 day course), also meds on MAR & form 6

Review d/c inform w/pt (form 6) Give pt copies. Ensure & document pt has way home

Ensure social service consult completely

Place original SA forms 1-6, photos, and address in small manila envelope to be placed in chart then in SA drawer for review (NEVER in kit or fridge).

Place appropriate yellow copies in kit. Have another RN review kit for accuracy. Seal w/ biohazard evidence seals—initial/date (save extra seal in drawer). Complete chain of evidence on kit (put pts name only if reported). No staples (rips gloves in crime lab). Never put kit in evidence bag! Place in locked fridge.

Fax crime report (mandatory Mass law, MGL 112) Office of Public Safety & to city where occurred, new Mass law to doc if EC given.

Lock chart in s/a drawer. Give blue copies to BS to d/c & remove flag from tracking

Call police to pick up kit (don't give name if not reported)

Complete s/a log. Doc nam/badge # (logs have been subpoenaed)

QA staff: is documentation appropriate (RN MD SS?)

MD staff: use this form s/p assault/exposures for d/c dx

Confidential—for peer review only. Not part of the medical record.

*   *   *

Another woman joins, a volunteer from the Boston Area Rape Crisis Center. I don't remember her name. She's in her early twenties, light brown hair up in a bun. She has a black, light coat on. Her role is to be a kind human during the rape kit procedure—a simple, indispensable presence.

"I have something for you." She grabs a plastic bag from her coat. In it: a pair of black-and-white underwear. "Since they take your underwear as a part of evidence collection, I have a new pair for you."

She continues. "On the topic of reporting, I know it's overwhelming, but there is an option of submitting a Jane Doe kit. It means your name won't be attached to it, but your evidence will still be taken. It won't initiate a police report. You will have fifteen years to initiate. I know it's a lot to take in, but by the end of this rape kit you'll have to make a decision."

My career was my safety net to run away from that terrible place I escaped from. I'm not ready to cut that net away—to let this rape derail the rest of my life.

"I want a Jane Doe kit," I say.

* * *

FORM 6 COMMONWEALTH OF MASSACHUSETTS SEXUAL ASSAULT EVIDENCE COLLECTION KIT

KIT NUMBER XXXXX

Antibiotics

Antiemetic

Emergency Contraception Offered (Must be offered if woman is of childbearing age)

Tetanus Toxoid

Hepatitis B prevention

HIV prevention medication
Additional medication

PATIENT DISCHARGE INSTRUCTIONS
Please follow these important instructions below. Bring
these instructions to all of your doctor's appointments.

What was I seen for?
    You came to the BWH Emergency Department with Sexual
Assault. You have: *Assault*
    The following category of lab tests were performed
during your visit:

Complete Blood Count
Liver Function Tests
Chemistry Studies
Microbiology Tests
Pregnancy Tests

    You will receive a call from the infectious disease
clinic for follow-up. Return here if you have any new
symptoms or concerns.

Start These New Medications
    RALTEGRAVIR 400 mg by mouth two times a day for
28-day course
    USES: Raltegravir is used with other HIV medications
to help control HIV infection. It helps to decrease

the amount of HIV in your body so your immune system can work better. This lowers your chance of getting HIV complications (such as new infections, cancer) and improves your quality of life.

SIDE EFFECTS: Headache, nausea, dizziness, tiredness, or trouble sleeping may occur. If any of these effects persist or worsen, tell your doctor or pharmacist promptly. Remember that your doctor has prescribed this medication because he or she has judged that the benefit to you is greater than the risk of side effects.

TRUVADA (EMTRICITABINE/TENOFOVIR) 200 mg/300 mg, 1 tablet by mouth daily. This is a partial fill of a 28-day course.

USES: This product is used with other HIV medications to help control HIV infection. It helps to decrease the amount of HIV in your body so your immune system can work better. This lowers your chance of getting HIV complications (such as new infections, cancer) and improves your quality of life.

SIDE EFFECTS: Nausea, vomiting, diarrhea, headache, dizziness, trouble sleeping, back pain, or change in the color of skin on your palms or soles of your feet may occur.

COMPAZINE (PROCHLORPERAZINE MALEATE) 100 mg by mouth every 6 hours for 4 days

．　．　．

It's been around six hours. Dr. Obermeyer stops by.

"What do you want me to write for your schoolwork extensions?" he asks.

I shrug. All I can think about is how I have to graduate. How I have to make it out.

"I don't know," I say.

"Let's start with a month. If you need more, just let me know."

. . .

BRIGHAM AND WOMEN'S HOSPITAL
10/14/2013 7:01 AM

SCHOOL RESTRICTION NOTE
Amanda Nguyen was seen in the BWH Emergency Department on the above date and may return to school with the following restrictions: Please grant Amanda an extension for home assignments for one month.

Clinician's Signature

Electronically signed by Ziad Obermeyer, MD, MPhil, on 10/14/2013 7:01:32 AM

. . .

THE HOSPITAL

PAYMENT OVERVIEW
HEALTH PLAN PAYMENT BREAKDOWN

10/14/13	Emergency Room	$2,598.00
10/14/13	INJ/Immunization	$242.16
10/14/13	IV Therapy	$235.00
10/14/13	Pharmacy	$171.42
10/14/13	Immunology	$138.00
10/14/13	Chemistry	$131.00
10/14/13	Immunology	$124.00
10/14/13	Immunology	$123.00
10/14/13	Bacteriology	$122.00
10/14/13	Laboratory	$94.00
10/14/13	Laboratory	$74.00
10/14/13	Urology	$35.00
10/14/13	Laboratory	$16.00
10/14/13	Hospital Services	$7.21
10/14/13	Clinic	$350.00
10/14/13	Emergency Dept SVC	$403.00

Grand Total: $4,863.79

•   •   •

I am handed many pamphlets. Some of the assortment includes:

Victim Rights Law Center
Emergency Contraception after Sexual Assault: Five Key
    Facts for Survivors
Sexual Assault & HIV/AIDS

List of Rape Crisis Centers and Hotlines in
    Massachusetts
The Massachusetts Victim Bill of Rights
Contact Information for: Massachusetts' District
    Attorneys & Victim Witness Program Directors
Forensics for Survivors
Boston Area Rape Crisis Center
Legal Referral Services
Notice: How Medical Information About You May Be
    Used and Disclosed
Forensic Sexual Assault Exam Expense Application

The pamphlets for loved ones of survivors reads:

HER IMMEDIATE NEEDS

One of the most frightening experiences for a survivor
is getting the courage to talk to you and worrying how
you will react. Your reaction can set the tone for her
recovery in years to come. She will wonder,

"Will I need medical care?"

"Should I tell my family?"

"Should I report this to the police?"

"Could it happen again?"

"Will I become pregnant?"

"What if I get a disease like AIDS?"

"Will others reject me now?"

"Am I ruined for the rest of my life?"

"Will I be an embarrassment to the people I love?"

"Can my life be normal again?"

Clearly, rape isn't something she can just "get over." The emotional effects can last for years, and unfortunately some helpers like police, doctors, ministers, and lawyers can be insensitive. For example, if she reports the assault to a hospital, they will collect physical evidence to be used in convicting the attacker. This is an intimate, painful process. And even more distressing is that this evidence must be collected before she bathes, changes clothes, eats, drinks, smokes, or brushes her hair. If the rape has just happened, you should encourage her to seek medical help, but the decision should remain hers.

*   *   *

At 7:15 a.m. I walk back out to the front desk. There is a new attendant—maybe both of us are new now. She hands me a taxi voucher to go back to the dorm room where I was raped only hours ago. I have never more fully understood the definition of loneliness than I do at this moment. In my abject despair, a fire starts burning.

This rape, I tell myself, *will not be the end of my dreams. I will get through this.*

Sixty-five pieces of paper, including pamphlets, brochures, and discharge instructions were given to me throughout the night. On one of the sixty-five pages is an unassuming sentence I don't see right away—a simple string of words that will go on to shape the course of my life: "At the end of six months, it will be destroyed." The *it* is my rape kit. Or perhaps the *it* is me. Because untested kits, especially Jane Doe ones, are systematically destroyed by the Commonwealth of Massachusetts every six months.

I can't hear it yet, but the countdown clock begins.

5.

The First Helper

The edges of the cave reveal themselves in the torch-light. The walls are turning, transitioning from cold, smooth gray to rough, red sandstone. This new rock is made up of millennia-old calcified sand dunes, each wall revealing layers of brilliant and deep colors: yellows, oranges, browns, and purples.

We enter a labyrinth of narrow slot canyons now, carved by centuries of water. The walls stretch about five flights up, and beams of light radiate down from the opening at the top of the canyon. I don't need the torch anymore.

22 picks up 5 in her arms. The rest of us walk single file. Our footsteps are softened by the sand, but unmistakably I hear steps that are not ours.

"Hello? Anyone there?" My voice echoes.

As I turn the corner, I hold myself and brace for contact with a stranger.

A hiker stands in a small clearing in the middle of a sun-ray's beam. She has a brown cap on, a heavy-duty forty-gallon backpack with camping gear hanging off multiple colorful carabiner clips. In her hand are two trekking poles.

"Hi there!" She waves eagerly. "Isn't it beautiful?" She points her walking stick up at the sunlight. Her face scrunches up; she squints her eyes and takes a closer look at us. "You lost?"

"Yes. We are. And we need help," I say.

15 points at 5, who is slumped over on 22's shoulders. "Do you know how we can get to a healer?"

"Oh dear." The hiker bites her lips. "Yes, I do. It's kind of hard to get out of these canyons, but I do have something that can help you navigate."

"What can we offer you?" I ask, and the stranger smiles.

"How about a memory? Why don't you tell me the story of your first helper?"

We look around. "You tell it, 15," says 22.

"Okay."

15 begins to tell her story.

• • •

"The stars were my first protectors."

As 15 talks, we are all drawn into the vista of her memory—living it in tandem, again, or for the first time.

Orion's belt twinkles in the clear spring night sky above

us. Beneath the stillness of the cosmos, 15 is there, frantic, in a pink hoodie, panting as she's sprinting down the asphalt streets of suburban Southern California. Cookie-cutter houses line the concrete sidewalk. A fork in the road lies ahead. Without slowing down, 15's head whips left, then right. A split-second decision. She chooses the right, headed toward the neighborhood park. What could she be running away from?

15 keeps running, and looking behind her we see our house at the end of the street. The sound of plates crashing. We know it's Dad.

"When he entered one of his violent episodes," 15 tells us, "there was nothing that could bring him back. Mom and I used to stay at the local public library until closing hours—until he figured out that's where we went. Dad had no public filter. He'd scream and yell in the library, too. So we switched to a Barnes & Noble in the neighboring town. He found us there. When it got bad, we'd go next to the horse ranches in Norco. Mom would tell me to wait while she went back first to try to calm him down. I would count the stars in the sky while I waited. That's how I first fell in love with the stars.

"Some kids have pencil marks on the walls of their home—a reminder, year by year, of how tall they've grown. My home had patches—patches that grew over time, corresponding to the size of my head at every age where his hands drove me into the plaster.

"'Only God can take away your brain,' Mom used to say. Which is why she let him bruise me everywhere but drew the line at my head. My mother would bargain with my father and tell him to hit me 'anywhere but the head.' That did not stop him. Dad would take my long hair and whip it against the wall. I can have long hair today, and it will not be leveraged against my body to smash me into violence.

"Mom urged me to use education as a way to escape—a way out that she had closed to herself long before. Perhaps she felt that if she hadn't quit her education, things could have been different. It was Dad who convinced Mom to drop out of school. She had been the first woman in her family to make it into higher education, before the fall of Saigon prevented her from graduating college in Vietnam. Once she made it to America, she enrolled at Cal State Fullerton to complete her engineering degree. Then she met him. He was a teaching assistant and offered to tutor her. She took his advice—to drop out, to leave the workforce, to stay at home."

●　●　●

15 sits alone in the park. She's on a bench, pink hood up, hugging her legs. Her face is tilted up to the night sky, tears streaming down. She's mumbling something, counting the stars. Back on Earth, a pair of headlights breaches the blackness, then switches off.

Mom steps out of the car.

"Amanda, I got the bags. Let's go," she says in Vietnamese.

●　●　●

"To the rest of the world," 15 tells us, "Mom projected the perfect image of idyllic family life. Mom needed everyone to like her. Even Dad. My academic excellence aided her image, her calculated perception of self-worth. 'Như hình như bóng' was how she'd describe us. 'Like a shadow to an image.' I was an extension of her.

"She was the closest thing to an ally I had to survive, even if it was to serve her own needs. Anything I ever achieved was never my own. I was constantly reminded that I achieved things only because she let me do them under the fragile terms of his abuse. Being extraordinary was a method of survival, a literal way to avoid the violence for a brief moment, to weave a lifeline to opportunities to be outside the home so that one day I could leave. It was an unsustainable Faustian bargain. But to a child, alone, in a horror house, it was all that I could strive toward.

"The one person Mom could be honest with was Y Ut, her younger sister. Both were refugees on the same boat. They survived hell together. 'We went into death to seek life,' they'd tell me. Except Mom's hell never stopped.

"Safety tastes like Dreyer's cold hard vanilla ice cream. So hard it makes your spoon bend. Y Ut's home was the first place I didn't have to be constantly vigilant. Every time Mom took me to hide at Y Ut's, my aunt would have a scoop of ice cream waiting for me and put *Scooby-Doo* on the TV. She lived in Anaheim, forty minutes from where we lived in Corona. Enough time to plan an escape if Dad wanted to come. Y Ut's condo had two exits. There was the front door, and then there was the garage in the back that opened up to a different street. If Dad came in the front of the house, we could sneak out the back.

"Do all daughters fall into the same fate as their mothers? If so, my version is that I avoided my fate thanks to Y Ut, who would become my safe haven. When it came time to apply to college, Dad forbade me. Y Ut would be a co-conspirator in my escape to freedom, to Harvard. I ran away from home to apply to college. I hid at her condo. My father tracked me and tried to break down the door. My uncle, Duong Ut, stood in the doorway and protected me."

* * *

15 is silent, still wiping away tears on the sleeve of her hoodie.

She sees that her bags are packed. Maybe this time is different. Mom is headed to the freeway. We're actually doing this. Maybe we're going to Y Ut's home.

Something has changed in Mom's face. She misses the exit to Anaheim.

The car swerves. Click. The doors are locked.

A horror dawns.

She turns the car around. We are heading back.

"Why did you turn back? Where are we going?"

Mom remains silent.

"You can't take me back there! How can you?!"

"It'll be better. I can talk to him."

"No no no NO. NO!" 15 screams uselessly into the void as she pulls repeatedly at the locked car handle. "You can't do this to us! You can't do this to me. How can you live like this?"

"You don't know what it's like. How bad it was in Vietnam. Family must stay together."

"We're not in Vietnam anymore!"

"Family must stay together."

The sun has started to rise on the trail. The stars are no longer twinkling.

• • •

"Thank you," the hiker says. She shakes her body as if to readjust. "Y Ut is really special."

"At least Mom thought we could get into Harvard," says 15.

"That doesn't excuse her for what she did," 22 immediately snaps.

"Hey, both things can be true, but let's focus on why we're here. You said you had something for us?" I say to the hiker.

"I do. But first, I need you to know what's ahead of you. Along this walk, there are five realms. Each realm is kept by a helper to aid you on your path to find the healer. Each helper will bear a gift. And each will seek a memory in exchange."

The hiker plops her backpack down to the ground, unzips it, and reaches within.

"This is my realm. My gift to you is this compass." The hiker places it in my hands.

The compass is weighted. It looks like an antique made from brass and glass. Engraved in italics on the top of the compass are these words:

Hope from Denial

"When you have hope, the compass will point you to what it is you hope for."

"Okaaay," I say skeptically as I turn it over. I trace the engraved words with my thumb. "And Denial?"

"That would be me. I am Denial—your first helper."

"How do we know where to go next?" 22 asks.

Denial lifts her hands and taps at the compass. "You must find Anger."

6.

HOW TO SURVIVE THE IMMEDIATE AFTERMATH OF A RAPE: A GUIDE

STEP 1: DO LAUNDRY

The taxi drops me off back in front of my dorm, Kirkland House. Back to where I was raped. People joke that Harvard is like Hogwarts, but they're not far off. Each of its twelve houses harbors its own singular culture, its own distinct rituals, and even its own specific architecture. Kirkland is one of the smallest houses, home to several hundred people: just small enough that everyone knows everyone. It has a colonial-style dining hall, a quaint library, and a grandiose common room—the kind of ostentatiously pretentious chamber that is exactly what people think of when they conjure up an image of Harvard. Dark, polished mahogany walls are framed by crimson velvet drapes. A grand piano sits adjacent to a sizable fireplace. The Kirkland crest is carved directly into the wood of the wall. Corinthian columns bask in the glow of golden chandeliers. Bloodred, navy blue, and pin-striped wingback chairs dot the matching Persian rugs. An oil portrait of a nineteenth-century house "master" in what looks like a full Regency tailcoat hangs in the middle of the wall, his judgmental gaze bearing down on you no matter where you stand in the room. This place defines prim and proper. Nothing untoward or unspeakable is supposed to happen here.

Forty short paces separate the gate where I've been dropped off from the entrance to my room, but right now it feels like a chasm. I don't want to go back.

In movies, they never depict the logistics after the trauma. Action heroes fight, shit happens, and we jump to the next scene. We never see the bandages get changed, the car get repaired, or the laundry get done. But in real life, you don't get to skip ahead. And at this moment, a small pile of laundry feels like Everest to me—an insurmountable mountain that somehow has to be scaled.

Someone observing me from the outside would have described me then as a person still rendering. A spin cycle trapped in an endless orbit. A basketful of delicates never quite clean. My body and soul hurt in places I didn't know could hurt. I was numb on the outside, rooted to the ground—immobile, dazed, stunned. Thick paperwork still in my hand, the rape crisis counselor's new underwear still on my body, a hospital band still wrapped around my wrist. Willing myself to wash the bedsheets I was raped on. To wash away the worst night of my life.

In my rendering, I am imagining scenarios to prepare for. *How do you tell people? How do you pick up the pieces from a life that's suddenly shattered? Where do you start?*

I find myself grateful that it's early in the morning. No one is awake for me to run into. No friend to casually say, "Hey! How are you?"

What would I even say? "I've just left the hospital. I've just been raped."

I need to move. I need to move out of the cold. Just take one step. Just one step. And then another one.

There you go.

Now one more.

There you go.

One foot in front of the next.

I stop in front of my entryway door.

I can't go in by myself. I am not strong enough. The sun is rising, and it won't be long before the whole house springs to life with people heading off to breakfast in the dining room. Especially the athletes who have to get to practice. I don't have long.

Who is up this early? Who can help? More importantly, who would understand the crushing weight of this moment?

Alex can.

Alex, my Kirkland housemate, was fourteen years old when he survived a drive-by shooting in Los Angeles. In high school, Alex was in a gang. While at a local burger joint with his brothers a rival gang spotted them. As he and his friends walked out of the restaurant bullets sprayed out of a white Honda Civic. One of the bullets found its way into Alex's friend. Alex held his friend in his arms as he gave his last breath. After that he quit the gang, rebuilt his life, and eventually found himself at Harvard living in Kirkland House. Years later he would return to LA to become an educator, working on gang rehabilitation and helping kids just like him.

Alex would understand.

I hear his thuds running down the stairs as fast as he can after receiving my text to meet me in front of my door. Kind eyes. Black hair. Usually a laughter that bellows. His eyes dart to my hands.

The metal of the keys presses in my palm. They make red marks digging into my fists. I realize I've been gripping them with white bare knuckles. Shaking. He opens his palm and lifts it toward my closed fists.

"We can open the door together," he offers.

I nod in silence. I place the keys in and twist. He stands next to me and pushes the door. We walk across the creaky, shiny hardwood floors, meticulously polished in a vain attempt to cover up the scratches of previous tenants. I place the heaps of paperwork and brochures down, along with the large orange pill bottles that contain my HIV prophylaxes. Alex stands with me in my dorm room.

"I can't sleep in this. I can't. I can't." My voice is slightly above a whisper; I can barely muster enough breath for the words to escape my throat. I'm rendering again.

"I'll wash your sheets with you," he tells me.

Alex peels off the first corner of the sheet. The other corners bounce together like they couldn't come off fast enough. He crumples the blue-and-white sheet into a gray hamper bag. I know he deliberately used the words "with you" to make me feel like we're doing this together, but truly he's doing all the work. I am numb, frozen still, and it's all I can do to whisper thank-you as he quietly tends to the scene.

Alex carries the hamper in his left arm and pushes the door with his right, and I follow behind him in a trance as he walks down to the basement laundry room—blessedly empty at this early hour. He stuffs the sheets in, gently presses the door shut, puts the coins in. One by one the quarters clang. The machine starts tumbling.

We stand for what seems like an eternity in silence. Watching the tumbling, of the sheets, of life.

I'm still rendering. Pieces of this moment carom through my memory like laundry in the machine—the rumble of the appliance; the starkness of the concrete floor; the laundry room's humidity.

Most of all I remember Alex's kindness.

In stereotypical movies, the gallant hero saves the damsel in distress through daring dramatic action. He slays the dragon. He walks through fire. He beats back the villains at the door.

In real life, heroes wash your sheets with you. Heroes hug

you. In the dark, damp, gray laundry room, Alex holds me in his arms. I know what his arms have held before. Another friend who could not be saved. But this time, his arms do save his friend's life. His arms save mine.

STEP 2: BECOME A HOUSE BUM

For a week I don't leave my room.

Survivors bear no responsibility for the violence that happens to them—but the world makes every effort to place the burden on us regardless. There is no length societies will not go to, no absurd logical leap people won't take, to recast our simple, human act of survival as something dirty and shameful.

I bled for myself each time a person or institution assumed that I'd been asking for it—either out loud or by quiet implication. And I bled for survivors around the world, whose experience of victim-blaming manifested as honor killings. Families, in a woefully misguided attempt to protect their shared sense of dignity, murdering their own daughters, sisters, or wives who had been raped. I thought of what my father would think, a man who already thought I was dishonorable in so many different ways. Would he kill me, too?

My mind could not stop replaying the events of the rape over and over. *How did this happen?* My firsthand knowledge of the truth, my feminist credentials, my basic self-awareness—none of it mattered in those first brutal days. Society and its conditioning won out, and I found myself questioning myself with suspicion. *Why me? What did I do wrong? Why can't I just get over it? When will I stop feeling this way—like my insides are lacerated? Like my spirit is irreparably broken?*

Rape is rape is rape is rape. End of story. But even for many of us who live through it, it takes time to get to that understanding and acceptance. Years, for some. Only a week, thankfully, for me. In that one week I do not leave my room. Time blurs; the hours tangle themselves together like dirty laundry waiting to get clean. My mind keeps cycling the same questions, to no avail. *Why did he rape me? Why me? Why did he rape me? Why?*

"Why?"

I would cry myself into exhaustion. I wouldn't drift asleep—I would pass out. Wake up crying again. Rendering. I look motionless on the outside, but a war is raging inside my head. Behind my eyes, my mind is in the trenches. The mental battle of guilt being fought over streams of self-blame, in fields of shame.

People think about the physical damage in a rape. The bruises, the tears. But the worst part is inside. In the cages of our mind that society has built for us. Patriarchal conditioning builds a scaffolding around our thoughts toward shame—directing them, framing them, stunting their growth. The war we fight lasts much longer than the physical act of rape.

After 168 hours—10,080 minutes—of asking the same one-word question over and over between lapses of awareness, I arrive at an answer.

The answer shows up like a cloud I have to catch: impossibly distant at first, but slowly rolling in with greater form and clarity. And the answer, of course, is that there is no answer to *why?*—no acceptable answer, at least. There is no truth to be found in the mind of a rapist; there's no logic there to be parsed or decoded. There is no world in which rape is okay, in which the question can be asked and answered, in which any sort of an explanation can be won, in which understanding can be found.

I am not a rapist. Therefore I cannot understand it. I concede that the cycle of *why?* will bring me nowhere.

The loop breaks.

STEP 3: MAKE A PROMISE TO YOURSELF

The bruises hurt. Purple, blue, and green swirls warp around my thighs. They look alien. I don't recognize my own skin. I have so many pills to take. They are blue and pink, hard to pronounce, overwhelming. So many. The HIV prophylaxis, which is part of the rape kit, makes me throw up. I am cycling again—this time in a loop from the toilet bowl to the porcelain sink. After wiping away my mouth I return to my room.

On the corner of my desk sits a leather notebook gifted by a friend. I rip out a page and make a promise to myself. In black ink I write, "Never Never Never Give Up." I tape it to my computer monitor to remind myself that I will not let him win. I will not let this rape prevent me from graduating.

STEP 4: BE A MASTER AT AWKWARD RESPONSES

How do you tell people the worst news of your life? As a species, we're well-equipped to celebrate, but we haven't evolved to gracefully share and receive horrific news. The best among us rarely know what to say, how to look, how to be there for a friend who is enduring something unendurable. We grimace, we frown, we shake our heads. We sigh, we cry, we hug. We dare to ask, "Are you okay?" with the best of intentions. But deep down, I think we know that nothing will suffice—there is no truly appropriate response to news this spiritually annihilating.

Mark is the first to get me out of my room. Mark is the best in our class. Incredibly organized. Everything comes easy to him, but being there for a friend who was raped—not even he knows what to do. But still, he tries—he tries to be there for me, and I learn quickly that the trying itself matters. In the absence of answers, it actually *is* the thought that counts.

"Ice cream makes everyone feel better," he says. I don't feel like eating. I just want to be with someone. He brings me to J.P. Licks, a busy, loud, popular ice cream store in Harvard Square. I find a corner to hide in.

"What do you want?"

"You decide. I just want to sit here in the corner."

J.P. Licks is the absolute antithesis of how I feel inside. It is neon bright. Fake green moss covers every wall to make it seem cheery, even in the chill of the winter. The refrigerators are Barbie pink, with words like "Cow Paws" in Comic Sans. Three chandeliers hang from the ceiling. Not regal and golden, like the ones in Kirkland House—these are more like glowing udders. A huge sign depicting a smiling, neon pink cow hangs over the door. Pop music blares. The vibes are goofy. The people around us are happy. It is an absurd place to grapple with desolate feelings. But maybe that's what I need.

Mark comes back with a cup of hot chocolate. I don't really like chocolate. But at that moment, it at least provides a sensation—a small, sweet contrast to the bitter metal coursing through my throat. We sit in silence for some time. Mark opens his mouth, then closes it, the wave of a comforting thought cresting and breaking before it can spill out into words. But I don't need him to say anything. I just need a friend to hold space. So we sit there in silence, nursing our hot chocolates underneath the neon cow sign.

•   •   •

Josh is the hardest to tell. He is part of the same club my rapist and I were in. I never went back to a meeting after my rape. I couldn't face the thought that a friend of mine might choose to remain friends with a rapist—my rapist. I didn't have the heart to find out some of my friends' true characters.

I never wanted revenge, not then, and not now. I wanted only to survive. I wanted only to make it stop hurting. But Josh finds out through the grapevine and reaches out to me to see if we can meet up; he is the first mutual friend of both me and my rapist to do so. So I agree. He asks me how it happened and is stunned by my story. I think a part of him wanted to hear it straight from me. It's one of the most painful parts of recovery: navigating your relationships with friends who know your rapist. Confronting the reality that someone we think is our friend has the capacity for this kind of violence. Even though they're neither survivors nor perpetrators themselves, these people face a reckoning, too. They have to choose who they are: someone who continues a friend-ship with a rapist or someone who denounces that behavior. I grew tired of explaining myself—of searching for the right words to describe something indescribable. So I show him my bruises instead. They are still enormous, sickly, domi-nating my skin. Josh stops in his tracks immediately. I wish I didn't need to show them in order to be believed. I don't know if he ever talked to my rapist again. But I know that he believed me.

• • •

Eventually I start venturing out again. Brent, a graduate stu-dent, is hosting a small dinner party for six people. Brent's home is beautiful. It's a townhouse with cascading light from an enormous glass window. The guests are other academics in the area. We're all helping him finish preparing the meal. Steak, noodles, salad. As Brent is guiding me toward his kitchen my stomach drops. Standing above a boiling pot of water is a tall, svelte man. I know him. That's Ziad. Dr. Ziad Obermeyer, the physician from the ER when I was admitted for my rape kit. I want to run, but I know at once that doing so is useless. What excuse could I even make up?

"Do you want to help with the salad?" Brent asks while holding up a tomato next to his face, smiling.

I wash the vegetables furiously. Something to keep my mind away. It does not work.

Shit shit shit. Will he say something? At this point, I have not shared what happened to me with everyone. Brent doesn't know. And these strangers at the dinner party don't know. I don't want them to know. I just want to have a normal night with friends. The tomato in my hand bursts under the running water.

I try to hide it. I see him looking at me. *Fuck, he knows.* I'm laser-focused on chopping a cucumber now. The conversation is buzzing all around me. People getting to know one another. Where are you studying? How do you spend your time? The luxury of small talk, of levity, of an evening unencumbered by the weight of something unspeakable. I am not engaging with anyone. Just slicing. My mind races. *Okay, next, grind the pepper.* I try to breathe with the pace of my slices. Box technique. Four counts in. Four counts hold. Four counts out. Four counts hold. Eventually all the meals are placed. People have gathered around the table. So has Ziad. There is no hiding. I must present my creation.

"What a beautiful salad!" Brent exclaims.

We sit down around the table—and of course my seat is directly across from Ziad. Our eyes meet like hot wires. I dart mine away to the table setting. Suddenly the fork is so interesting.

"All right, we're all here! I've brought you from all corners of my life. Does anyone know each other?" Brent asks.

Fuck fuck fuck. Will Ziad answer? I know he knows. But I also know HIPAA constrains him from saying that yes, in fact we know each other. We met while I was on a gurney, in Brigham and Women's Hospital.

My gaze meets Ziad's. I try to beg him with my eyes, with the smallest movement of my head to shake no.

"No," Ziad says, breaking his gaze to meet Brent's. I breathe a sigh of relief.

It's true that we've met. But we haven't truly met. We were doctor and patient then—not human and human. The person he might have met that night wasn't there, in her body, to be met.

Dinner begins. The cutlery clangs. The salad is served.

* * *

Surviving the aftermath of a rape will be different for everyone. Mine was laundry coming clean. Hot chocolate under the gaze of a bright pink cow. Timing my breath to the rhythmic slicing of a vegetable. It was friends who held space; it was friends who filled the silences. It was friends who couldn't understand until they saw. It was hours coming untangled and questions I learned to let go. Most of all, it was a promise to myself to keep going—a promise I would teach myself to keep.

7.

Finding Anger

The compass glows in my hand.

"Ah, we've got a lead! Follow me." Denial skips off through the slot canyon, the narrow walls echoing her colorful carabiners as they chime against one another. As we turn the corner, the crevasse opens into a flat vermilion desert road. The reddish pigment of the earth contrasts against a clear blue sky. Parked with the engine humming, an egg-yolk yellow taxi waits. Our eyes adjust to the scorching sunlight that illuminates the vista—a wash of primary colors melting together in the sky. Denial has already made it to the taxi while we are catching up.

As the window slowly rolls down, we see our driver. First his black chauffeur hat appears, then brown eyes, then a relaxed smile framed by a gray salt-and-pepper beard. If he stood up he'd be easily over six feet tall. His crisp white gloves and clean suit are prim and proper—he'd fit right into any painting on the wall back at Kirkland House.

Denial's cheeriness clashes with the driver's stoic air. She leans into the window chatting with him. As we catch up to her, soothing classical music and a bracing jet of air-conditioning pour out from the car.

"This is my friend Mr. R. He has agreed to take you to Anger's realm."

"With pleasure." Mr. R nods at us with a smile.

22, 15, and 5 climb into the back seat while I ride shot-gun. 5 sits in the middle.

"Thank you, Denial!" I yell through my open car window before I roll it back up. We watch her get smaller and smaller until she fades out of sight.

The road from Denial to Anger stretches out far on the horizon. Every time we crest a hill, there is only more road in its wake. Two lanes pierce the desert. One to go forward, the other to return. We are the only ones out there on either path.

The desert has a serene beauty to it, and I find comfort gazing up at the endless sky. It's a welcome reprieve from the dark cave and narrow canyons we started out from, an "eye spa" I can bask in for a while that instantly relaxes me, giving me that *ahhhh* feeling. How ironic, given that we're headed to Anger's realm. I wonder what it will look like. Hot, I imagine—hence the desert. But there is life here; life finds a way. Cacti dot the road. An occasional tumbleweed rolls past in the wind. The dry heat is so strong that the air melts into waves.

Inside the car, the air-conditioning is blasting. The soft

notes from the calming classical radio station harmonize with the engine's purr. This duet combined with the car's gentle vibrations create the perfect setting for sleep. The three sitting in the back seat have dozed off.

Mr. R seems laser-focused on the highway. I don't want to disturb him, and I don't want to wake anyone up. My eyes slowly shut.

•　•　•

A bump in the road jolts my stomach. I groggily open my eyes. It's dusk. We must have driven for hours. When we crest the next hill, a long line of cars appears ahead of us. The two lanes have given way to eight rows, all clogged with traffic. More cars roll in behind us, boxing us in. The honking wakes up 5, 15, and 22.

"How'd we get here?" 22 groans. "So many people want to get to Anger."

More cars pile up. Ours inches little by little, jerking each time Mr. R brakes. A wave of motion sickness hits me. I clench my abdomen and look for a horizon—some fixed image of the world that I can fixate on to calm my nerves. But the sun has set, and we are stuck in the gridlock. There seem to be even more lanes now, all full of seekers desperate to inch forward.

Inch. Jolt. Inch.

The blaring honks are ceaseless. They drown out the sound of the radio. The lanes have lost their authority; cars are trying to cut each other off left and right, making a metal rat's nest of the path.

Inch. Jolt. Inch.

Smog has started to seep in through the vents. I lift the collar of my dress and tuck my nose and mouth under it as a makeshift mask.

Inch. Jolt. Inch.

The car to our left bumps into the car in front of it. The driver gets out of his Hummer pickup. Slams his door shut. The other driver does the same, and a screaming match ensues.

Inch. Jolt. Inch.

Blaring honks. People yelling. 5 covers her ears. The purple poison on her hands has deepened in color.

"Your hands are getting worse," says 22. "At this rate, we're never going to get to Anger in time."

Inch. Jolt. Honks. Yelling. Smog choking.

Too tired to respond, still holding my body together to suppress my motion sickness, I watch the drivers scream at each other in the traffic jam. Others behind them have now rolled down their windows to yell since the two drivers are holding up the lane. It dawns on me.

The compass had never stopped glowing.

"22, we're here. We're here. This is Anger."

Our heads all turn to Mr. R.

"It's you," I pronounce. "Mr. R? Mr. . . . Rage."

He smiles. "Anger's fine, miss. Whatever name you prefer."

"But you're so . . . calm?" 15 blurts out.

"I'm a reflection, miss," he answers. "A reflection of your rage. And I don't see you boiling over—I don't see you lashing out. Your rage is like so many women's: calm on the outside, a hurricane within."

"Why the fuck didn't you tell us? You could have helped us all this time?" 22 explodes.

"Want to get out of here?"

"YES," we all shout.

"I'll need a memory for that. Why don't you tell me when you were the angriest?"

5, 15, and I all look at 22, the angriest of all of us.

"This is mine to tell," she asserts.

• • •

22 begins.

"A man's story is written with a pen. His destiny is an earned creation, flowing parallel with time, of his own will.

"A woman's life story begins at the end, born and bred with a pain inherent, a choice deprived, her womb an hourglass written in slipping sand falling under the gravity of society's reproductive manifest destiny. A mandatory prescription. Forever she walks through it all, never reaching the end. A glorious illusion, never enough in the eyes of the world.

"I was born a mistake.

"I was supposed to be a boy. In the ultrasound, I held out my finger—the doctors thought it was a penis. Maybe I was flipping them off. My name was supposed to be Theodore. The entire baby shower was for Theodore. Everything blue. In Vietnamese culture, boys bring honor. Girls do not. My parents never let me forget that from my first breath, I was a disappointment. I was born guilty for the crime of simply existing."

As 22 continues, a heavy fog surrounds the car. When it dissipates, we have left the desert and the taxi is parked outside our childhood home, idling in the memory of the most painful moment of our life. Through the window we hear screams. 22 explains what is happening behind those walls.

"The night before I flew to Harvard, my parents fought again. I could hear my father slam my mom's body into the wall. Mom always told me to not fight back or get involved. But I'd had enough that night. The very last night was the last chance for me to intervene. I opened my bedroom door, marched into the living room, and summoned the strength to pull him off her. He swung his fist at me and missed. I swung back and did not miss. I lifted my arm to block another blow to my face. His impact hit my wrist instead, which radiated sharp pain.

"Mom screamed. She disappeared into the kitchen and came back with a knife, holding it at her own throat.

"'Stop fighting! I'll kill myself!' I was too angry to hear her. Seventeen years of pain, of bottled-up rage, unraveled and exploded in me. I was older now, not a helpless child. He tried to push me down, but for the first time in my life I could—and did—push back.

"The threat of the knife wasn't working. So that night I learned of a more gruesome way to end your own life. My mother began to bite off her own tongue. As a person's tongue severs, blood engorges their mouth, filling up their airways until they drown in it.

"Something clicked in me when I saw her mouth turn purple. Like a robot, I walked away from my father into the kitchen, picked up the home phone, and dialed 911. Just like that. Dad was shell-shocked that I called. When I was in high school, my father would taunt me. He would hit me and then throw the phone and dare me to call the police. 'You need my money to get through college.'

"It was my mother who ran for the phone and took it out of my hands, hanging it up in one motion. The police called back. She said everything was fine and hung up again. She was trying to protect him. I remember walking calmly past him into the cul-de-sac, sitting in the street, waiting for the police to come find me.

"When I have PTSD flashbacks, I see the flashlights of the paramedics flitting around me like fireflies. I hear him yelling at the police. I remember the officer, a woman, telling him that he should feel lucky to have a daughter like me. I remember the doors of the ambulance closing and seeing my childhood home receding through those ambulance windows. It was the last time I ever saw my home.

"The doctor gave me a cast for my arm at the hospital. Mom, still trapped in denial, brought my father into the room and acted like nothing was wrong. It was the angriest I've ever felt—the biggest betrayal I have ever felt from her. I flew to Harvard the next morning."

●　●　●

Mr. R takes off his chauffeur hat and puts it over his heart. A fog floods the scene again and we are back in Anger's realm, standing next to the taxi, straining our eyes against the bright daylight and the ocher of the desert. No other cars are in sight.

"I'm sorry, Amanda." He pauses. "Your anger is your pain. And your pain is your power. Anger drives us to places we can't imagine, both good and bad."

He throws 22 the keys. "There's a full tank of gas, water, and food in the trunk. Fuel is my gift to you. Take the car past the horizon to the end of the road. When you hit the river, find the floating market. There you'll find Bargaining."

"Where will you go?" 5 asks, looking around at the boundless emptiness that surrounds us.

"Oh, there are always others who drive this way. There are millions out there, looking for me, right now."

"Thank you, Anger," I say as we climb into the car, 22 at the wheel, and head off to the next stage of our journey.

8.

DISCOVERING THE COUNTDOWN

I've forgotten what hunger feels like. Not only for food. But for life. For the sun. For warmth.

If the wind could blow directly into my room, it would most likely whisk me away. I am a shell of who I used to be— the skeleton of a leaf, trodden and bent, dried and desiccated, trying vainly to smooth itself back into form.

It is early in the morning and I can't keep avoiding my desk. My eyes stare at the brochures and heaps of paper from the hospital stacked neatly within a teal plastic folder on my plywood desk. I'm paralyzed, anchored to the polished, scratched-up wooden floor. Rendering again. I stare at the folder. The folder stares back. We've entered into a staring contest. One I'm destined to lose.

I know that on those pages are the details of what happened to me—the brutal reality. I try to slow down time, to stretch the moment out forever, so that I never have to open the folder. If the pages are never read, then maybe I can just be Amanda. A student who loves the stars. A person who loves petting dogs. A girl who loves the transformation of autumn leaves as they traverse the colors of sunrise. Maybe, in this little dorm room, if I stare at this folder forever, I won't have to look at its guts, my guts, the painful words that mark so clinically what happened to me. If I don't make any movements, what lies on the other side of opening that folder may never come to pass. I know it's irrational, but I stay still for a while. It's just a folder. But it's a folder that contains a diagnosis—a truth waiting to plunge me back into the cold. It's just a folder. My real-life Pandora's box. I wonder if Pandora, too, had a staring contest with that cursed box the gods dropped on her desk.

My phone rings. It's the Boston Area Rape Crisis Center. My time is over. I must open the folder. The rape crisis center brochure sits on top.

My right eye twitches to hold back tears. Deep breath. I answer the phone. Two women are on the line with me. They complete the new client intake information. It's clinical. They explain the technicalities of being their client. In our brief fourteen-minute call, one statistic remains with me forever.

"We're sorry this happened to you. We want you to know that even though you have the right to move forward and pursue action, the conviction rate for rape is one percent."

For every one hundred rapes, only one person sees justice.

"More importantly," the other woman states matter-of-factly, "it takes an average of two to three years."

My stomach contracts into a tight ball. "Two to three y-years?" I stammer, my voice cracking.

I don't have two to three years. Who has two to three years? For a 99 percent failure rate?

"Yes, at the very least. And it is a difficult two to three years. I know this is hard to hear, but we want you to have all the information."

Were they . . . trying to discourage me from moving forward? The eye twitches don't work anymore. Tears have now escaped.

"And . . ." The other woman sighs before completing her sentence. "In those years, the trial is all-consuming. It often means taking extended leave from the workplace. Have you told your parents? Perhaps they can help with the legal fees, with the medical fees, you know, with being there for you."

No. No, I haven't told them. I need to succeed to survive them. I need my career path to be a pathway out. I may not still physically be *there*, but without the financial stability of a career, I haven't truly made it out yet. I can't let this rape derail my chances of survival. Justice or career. Are these really my choices?

I'm choked into a speechless stupor, unable to process the reality of the criminal justice system. The world spins even faster around me.

The intake staffers continue on. "You do have the option of pressing charges later. The statute of limitations for rape in

Massachusetts is fifteen years. That's good you got a rape kit. With your evidence, you can come back when you're ready."

Who is ever ready to set aside two to three years of their life? But that's right . . . I still have my rape kit.

"Let us know what you decide."

I thank the women on the line. I know they are just trying to be helpful, but their words feel like hot coals to my soul. How could these be my only options? The call was fourteen minutes long. Not even an episode of a TV show. Fourteen minutes to shatter any hope I had of justice. Not that I had high hopes in the first place. My rock bottom has found a new low.

As soon as the line disconnects, my knees reflexively come up and my back curls into them, arms clutching each other in a fetal position, my head in between my legs. The air has been punched out of me. My body trembles. With nothing left to give, the most unimaginable scream escapes me. It stutters like razor blades slitting upward and across my throat, a gaping wound that only justice could close. I don't know for how long I sob in that fetal position, how long I beg for God to come.

The afternoon sun has moved and my hair heats up. I lift my head, and when I look up, I see a blurry sign through swollen eyes. Taped on the monitor, I see it: "Never Never Never Give Up."

I vow to heed that promise to myself, to take control of what I can. But I feel a manic panic bubbling to the surface. A tug-of-war jostles in my mind. Two distinct parts of me struggle for control: a wild part consumed by outrage and an ordered part scrambling to figure out what to do next. My blood boils with indignation. My brain cools the system, determined to figure something out. I can still call around. Learn more about the process. See if it really does take two to three years for a trial. See if maybe there could be another way. I will myself to power through the rest of the teal folder—every cut, every truth, every word.

I feel my pulse race. My hands scramble to push out the mess of shiny brochures across the bedspread, to cover the very place where it happened. The guts of the folder are sprawled across my bed so I can examine everything I'll need to read.

Victim Rights Law Center. Emergency Contraception after Sexual Assault: Five Key Facts for Survivors. Sexual Assault & HIV/ AIDS. List of Rape Crisis Centers and Hotlines in Massachusetts. The Massachusetts Victim Bill of Rights. Contact Information for: Massachusetts' District Attorneys & Victim Witness Program Directors.

I start flipping through the mess. I figure I should start with the rape kit. Somewhere in here must be information about my kit, about where the DNA taken from my body can be found.

Forensics for Survivors. Boston Area Rape Crisis Center. Legal Referral Services. Notice: How Medical Information About You May Be Used and Disclosed. Forensic Sexual Assault Exam Expense Application.

Sixty-five pieces of paper. Where to start? I pick one and begin to read it line by line.

I pore over each sentence. The sun sets and I don't notice. The shadows move across my room as I obsess over every piece of knowledge I can find. Picking up each of the sixty-five documents from my bed to my desk and back again. With every piece of information I read, another piece of the puzzle falls into place—but the picture it reveals is grim. I feel at once more knowledgeable, more in control, and yet more overwhelmed and enraged. The tug-of-war continues.

Here are some things I learned:

For every six women, one is raped.

One in four college women are sexually assaulted.

Most rapists are serial rapists.

Every sixty-eight seconds, an American is sexually assaulted.

Fifty-five percent of rapes happen at or near the victim's home.

Fewer than 20 percent of rapes are reported.

For every one hundred women, ninety-nine will never see justice.

Thirty-three percent of women who are raped contemplate suicide.

Thirteen percent of women who are raped attempt suicide.

Seventy percent of rape or sexual assault victims experience moderate to severe distress, a larger percentage than for any other violent crime.

It dawns on me. I am one of these statistics now.

I turn to the internet to verify what I'm reading. At every turn, I find roadblock after roadblock to pursue justice.

Instead of answers, I find horror stories. Copies of vital medical records and police reports denied. Shortfalls and irregularities in every state; symptoms of a broken promise.

And then destiny arrives. My eyes land on that simple set of words that will define the rest of my life: "At the end of six months, it will be destroyed."

Untested kits, especially Jane Does, are systematically destroyed by the Commonwealth of Massachusetts every six months. Rape kits are destroyed before they can be brought forth as evidence.

Wait . . . what? I read the words again. And again. And again.

"At the end of six months, it will be destroyed."

Blood rushes to my head.

Wait, no. It can't be. This can't be true. I did the right things. I did the things they told me to do.

I am losing my mind. No—the government has lost *its* mind. How can this be the policy? They tell us to go to the hospital and go to the police. But when we do, we are met with a system that systematically destroys our evidence and annihilates our only shot at justice. We are nothing against them.

I feel powerless, invisible, betrayed for a second time. A million questions race in my mind: Why does the government destroy rape kits? This kit is my key to the doors of justice—how can it just be lost? What is the next step in the process? How long will that take? Will this derail my career? Will I have to go back to the home I finally escaped? Where do I go from here, and who can help me? What other crimes do they destroy evidence for? Is this the law in all of America? What about in other states? Should I have been raped somewhere else? Would another state save my rape kit for longer? How can different states justify completely different sets of rules?

And the most urgent question: *Wait—where is my kit?* Where is the DNA they took from my body? I don't even know where it is. I turn to Google and write down the number and address of every single forensic lab in Massachusetts.

My justice is in that evidence. In a world that never trusts the word of women—that never gives credence to our voices or our stories—I need that proof to avoid a "he said, she said" and make my case.

A switch flips in me.

I manically google how to extend the timeline for rape kits, how to preserve my own justice beyond a paltry and uncertain six-month window. But there's no answer to be found—no process to extend that fleeting window of justice. I look at the calendar. My heart skips a beat. How many days do I have left? I trace the bad math back to that night in the hospital. Five months and twenty-three days remain.

The worst thing that happened to me wasn't being raped. It was being betrayed by America's criminal justice system. Suddenly I am confronted with a ticking time bomb. A horror game that puts *Saw* to shame. A labyrinth to nowhere, a bureaucratic joke worthy of Kafka. And a failure rate of 99 percent—that's the punch line. It dawns on me, of course, that rape victims are never meant to win. We're not meant to survive this at all. If we make it through the rape without drowning in our own blood, law enforcement, the justice system, and America itself are there to finish the job. To quiet our voices and sever our tongues. To betray us a second time. That's what it means to be raped.

All I see is red. I am fuming with rage. I do not accept this. I do not accept this fate.

In the dead of night, I remember what hunger feels like. I remember, too, that at the bottom of Pandora's box remained one last thing: hope. Hunger for justice is my hope.

How can a dried-up leaf smooth itself back to life? It can't. But it can transform into something else. With the right heat, even a leaf can become a spark. My rage becomes a fire—to burn the system, to light the path, to forge a changed world out of the ashes of my pain.

9.

A Good Deal

It's just us four now in the car headed away from Anger to find Bargaining. 22 turns the radio off.

"I liked the classical music," I protest.

"What about pop?" 15 says, reaching from the back seat to turn the radio on again.

"Watch it! I'm the designated music chooser," I joke as I shift through the static of the radio stations to find a pop channel for her. I wonder if it'll play music from her time instead of mine.

22, clearly still on edge, shouts, "I'll give you all a snack from the trunk if you shut up!"

15 retreats back to her seat. All of us stop talking. 22 is still visibly shaken by the memory she gave to Anger.

A wound emerges from deep within my core. It spills out agony, blooming upward and outward.

I place my hand on 22's shoulders. "I know the pain—I lived it, too."

There's silence for a minute.

"Tell me the hurt stops, 30."

"It never does," I tell her. "But we learn to live with it. We find other love, from friends, from ourselves. We grow our hearts. The pain doesn't lessen in size, but with time passing and with more life to give love, it becomes less and less sharp than it is now."

"It's not fair."

"No, it isn't fair. But when fairness fails us, we still have the agency to create our own justice. The change we bring is the consolation prize for our grief."

22 takes her right hand off the steering wheel and intertwines it with my left hand. She squeezes it tight.

We ride together in silent understanding, knowing that throughout the pain we are never alone, that we have one another, every version of our past and future selves we'll ever be.

* * *

Bargaining's realm announces itself with sound before sight. The bobbing of boat engines on the floating river market harmonize with the buzzing street carts that line the river's banks. Underneath several hanging barbecued ducks, a butcher's steady chopping beats like a metronome. The fragrance of cooked meat wafts from sizzling grills. Trills of flash fires dance with hot oil crackles as blue fire peeks out over the curves of a wok. Noodle soups bubble away. There is rhythm in the chaos.

"How do we find Bargaining in all of this?" I wonder out loud as 22 parks the car. 15 unlocks the trunk to grab Anger's gift for us. We join her to look. A large forty-liter backpack is stuffed to the brim: big bottles of water weigh it down, while bread, bananas, and small snacks fill the rest of the bag. Fuel for our stomachs.

"22, you just drove us, and 15, you've been watching 5. I'll carry the backpack," I offer. "15 and 22, you take turns watching 5." I split the bushel of bananas and hand one to each of us. "Let's go find Bargaining."

The market's frenetic energy is an organism in and of itself. Hundreds of people conversing, boat merchants advertising their inventory of goods, street vendors pushing stainless steel carts of overflowing sweets, motorcycles weaving through pedestrians—like blood cells traveling through arteries. A stray brown dog runs right up to 5. It happily pants, tongue out, tail wagging.

"Aww! Can dogs eat bananas?" 15 breaks off a piece and waves it at the dog. It opens its mouth and takes it from her hand.

A makeshift flower stall catches my eye. Tiers of gorgeous white hydrangeas tower. Purple orchids drip from hanging baskets. Stems of red and orange roses burst from multiple vases. It is a kaleidoscope of blooms. I spot sunflowers and tulips, my favorites. Before heading to the flower stall, I look back at 22, 15, and 5 playing with the puppy. 22 looks genuinely cheerful. This is the first time we've been happy together. A light smile dances across my lips.

Up close the flower stall thrills me even more. Silk pastel-colored ribbons twist into little bows around arranged bouquets. Wicker baskets are lined up for customers to place their chosen flowers into. A wooden framed sign reads, "A dozen stems for a laughing memory."

Right—currency here in the land of memory is, of course, memories. I wonder what recollection I'd choose in exchange for the sunflowers. When we told Denial and Anger our stories, doing so didn't erase what happened. We still remember. But telling our story gave us a chance to share our knowledge, to process.

I peek through the rows of flowers to check in on the group. They're still laughing with the dog. Then panic grips me. There are only two. 15 and 22.

I drop the wicker basket in my hand and run toward them. "Where's 5?"

"What?" 15 says, her eyes still on the dog.

"Where is 5?!" I shout.

22 and 15 look up at me.

"Oh shit, shit," 22 says, looking around frantically.

"She was just here . . . a moment ago . . . She was playing with us, too . . ." 15 mumbles.

"How could you lose her!" I am furious.

"I thought 22 was holding her . . ." 15 says.

"Me? You have been the one babysitting her!" 22 retorts.

"Ugh, I take my eyes off you all for one second and she's missing! I should have stayed," I yell.

"Do we split up to find her, 30?" 15 asks.

I squash the idea. "No, no, we stay together. We won't be able to find each other on top of finding her if we split up."

We start by shouting for 5 and asking strangers for any sightings.

"Have you seen a five-year-old by herself?"

"5! 5!"

All three of us scream at the tops of our lungs, but still we barely break through the noise of the market. We run alongside the riverbank, dodging vendors and pedestrians. I pant on the pier at the end of the market, winded. 22 and 15 are also breathing heavily. The marina stretches outward into a vast body of water; the sea looks endless, stretching on forever. Hundreds of boats of all sizes—jet boats, fishing vessels, large sailboats—are coming in and out of the harbor.

Suddenly, a deep voice with a southern drawl addresses us: "Thanks for finding my dog."

We follow the voice to its owner. A gruff older gentleman in a navy captain uniform stands with the brown dog sitting at his feet. A pipe hangs out of his mouth.

"Have you seen a little girl that looks like us?"

"I have. 5, right?"

"Yes!" we shout in unison.

"She's on my boat."

"Can you bring us to her?" I ask.

"Yes, but you must give me a memory first. Come on, you know how this works."

"You want us to pay for our sister? Absolutely not, we don't negotiate with kidnappers!" 22 snaps.

"Who said anything about kidnapping?"

"Uh-huh, yeah, we believe that."

"Wait . . . are you . . . Bargaining?" 15 asks.

"Bingo."

"All right, how do we get 5 back?"

"Tell me the worst deal you've ever made."

I look over to 22, who is still weary from the last memory she gave. "I'll tell this one," I volunteer.

"Okay, go for it." Bargaining snaps his fingers, and we are transported back to Harvard, at the start.

• • •

In my memory, we stand in front of Matthews Hall, a freshman dormitory built in the 1800s with classic red bricks that define Harvard's architectural aesthetic. It's 2009. Matthews sits directly in Harvard Yard, a grassy twenty-two-acre area enclosed by freshman dorms and the grand marble Widener Library, home to three and a half million books on its shelves. Today is move-in day, the only day of the year when cars are allowed in the Yard. Students are exploring their dorms with their parents, who buy sweatshirts that proudly declare "Harvard Dad" or "Harvard Mom." This is a familiar scene, a rite of passage for many Americans. It's conventional, emotional, and proud.

Seventeen-year-old me stands on the steps of Matthews with a cast around my left hand. I've arrived fresh off the plane. Hours ago, after the most traumatic moment of my life, I was discharged from the emergency room and left straight for my flight.

"Who is that man with you?" Bargaining asks.

"That's the Harvard police officer assigned to protect me," I tell him. "I found out when I arrived that my father followed me from California. He couldn't bear letting me escape from his control. While people were saying goodbye to their parents, I was fleeing mine. Other students' first task was to buy school supplies. My first task was to have the University issue a restraining order in the form of a no-trespass order. Father would be arrested if he stepped on campus. Harvard was my first safe haven.

"This officer gave me my first tour of the campus. I will never forget his kindness. He told me where the Dalai Lama planted a tree, and where the arc of one building could amplify sounds to the right listener, or where this celebrity did this and that."

We watch my younger self follow the police officer around campus as he points out landmarks.

"Harvard was my first real home, but one that I couldn't leave because I would not be protected outside its walls. It was at once a safe haven and a prison. I became really, really good friends with the professors, janitors, and cafeteria chefs. I knew the best, most secret places at Harvard because of my knowledge from that police officer and from living at school the way I did. I knew all the lore, from ghost stories to myths, from my hours talking to the staff. Because of that, I gave the best tours at Harvard and became a favorite guide to the dignitaries who visited. One of the dignitaries I met was Ursula, whom I met at the Harvard Institute of Politics. I still struggled with the guilt of leaving my mother behind, even if she'd betrayed me. But I'll never forget how, after talking, Ursula told me, 'You can't save someone who doesn't want to be saved.'"

Bargaining takes out his pocket watch. We stand still in the middle of the yard, but the changes in our environment speed up around us. The hands on the watch spin as we jump through time. The tree's autumn leaves become brilliantly saturated, then shed to the ground.

The watch stops spinning. It's a winter wonderland. The yard is empty; the air is crisp. Our breath is visible. Beautiful mounds of fresh powdered snow are intersected by shoveled walking paths. Flakes fall gently from the sky around us. An eighteen-year-old me is twirling alone under the falling snow. I carve out my own joy amid it all.

"I always loved January break; everyone would be gone for the holidays for a month and only I would remain. It's when Harvard felt most like home. A friend would host me for a couple days or a meal during Thanksgiving or Christmas, but I returned to campus for safety. Because I stayed on campus during the breaks, my key card had staff access to all the common rooms. 'God Access.' It was so fun. I could explore. Harvard really was like Hogwarts, and I had the Marauder's Map. One of the kind people at Harvard was Cathy McLaughlin, the executive director of the Harvard Institute of Politics. She brought me home for Thanksgiving once. She also controlled JFK's preserved room in Winthrop House and let me live there. It's usually only reserved for heads of state when they come to Harvard, but since it was open, she let me stay. I felt like an orphan. Like Harry Potter. Cathy was my Dumbledore."

The clock speeds up again, and time stops on a fresh spring night. On the steps of Widener Library, a now truly college-aged me lies, staring up at the sky.

"My favorite thing to do at Harvard was stargazing on the steps of Widener Library," I tell Bargaining. "It reminded me how I used to count the stars to get by, waiting for my mother to come and get me when I'd run away. The stars kept my astronaut dreams still within my sights. Harvard meant so much to me. Which is why it was a shattering experience to be raped here. This was my only home. I had nowhere to go. Harvard was supposed to be my escape. I thought I'd traded my California home for a better, safer one. But instead this new home failed to protect me from the violence I'd tried to run from. Violence just came in a different form."

"That is a bad deal." Bargaining pauses. "I'll give you a better one."

He snaps his fingers, and we are back on the dock.

"5 is on my boat. Come with me."

We follow Bargaining down the massive dock. At the end is a sizable sailboat with a gorgeous crimson red sail shaped like the fin of a swordfish. It's a junk, a Southeast Asian ship with classic sails.

"This is my ship."

5 waves at us from the deck.

"5! We were so worried," 22 shouts as we all board hastily to hug her.

Through the crush of us squeezing her, 5 exclaims with a giggle, "I'm okay! Look! I found him. He told me he knows Spongebob."

15 pulls back from the group hug, but when she does she picks up 5's swollen hands. "They've gotten worse."

"Stop joking, 5. We were worried sick about you. You're clearly not okay. We need to get you to the healer as fast as possible," I say.

Bargaining takes off his captain's hat, places it on 5, and looks at me. "My gift to you is this ship, named after my dog. Take the compass Denial gave you and place it in the middle of the helm. It'll automatically take you across the Siren Sea to Sadness's realm."

"Siren Sea?"

"Yes, this body of water is . . . unique. Only look up to the stars above. Do not stare too closely at the water, and under no circumstances should you touch it. If you look too hard, the water shows our dreams. It will pull you in and drown you."

There's a round indentation in the helm. I press the compass into it—it fits perfectly. Bargaining steps back onto the dock and waves as we set sail. A sunset illuminates the horizon in brilliant hues of orange, magenta, and lilac. On the side of the boat, its name glistens in the reflecting water: *Spongebob*.

10.

BONOBOS

I live by the countdown clock now. It hangs over me, in every second, in every action. While I am in class. While I'm brushing my teeth. While I eat in the dining hall. While I'm studying in front of my computer. While I am around other people. All I hear are the thundering, ticking seconds that strike without mercy. The horizons of my life have shrunk. Everything I do is overwhelmed by the context of the clock. Every second that slips is a second less I have to save my rape kit, my justice, my future. My mind sprints in the dark, not knowing where to go. But I try anything to grab on to hope. Flailing, desperately, like a body trying to gasp for air as it drowns. I am drowning—but below the surface, no one can hear my cries.

All my senses have been turned on high alert. I am perpetually on edge. I have spent the last week cold-calling and emailing every forensic lab I can find in Massachusetts, exhausted by an endless loop of conversations about my rape kit—conversations to nowhere. And yet, I press on, stubbornly trying to save my evidence.

A simple phone exchange with the Boston Area Rape Crisis Center to confirm whether rape kits are actually destroyed in Massachusetts sends me spinning. At first, the staff person assures me that rape kits are not destroyed. The next day, they call back to correct themselves and say they *are* destroyed. Then another person from the center calls, indicating that maybe they are wrong again. I hang on to every morsel of hope, but the whiplash of each passing call puts me into a catatonic state, complete with hyperventilation, a racing heart, another hour of sobbing to complete each interaction. There is no room for nuance. I am stuck in flight, fight, or freeze. But this time, at last, with my persistence, I am fighting back.

I need to talk to someone who knows what I'm going through. I need to talk to a rape survivor. The first person who told me that they were raped was a classmate of mine at Harvard named Melanie. Months before my own attack, Melanie shared with me what happened to her. She didn't tell me the details, and I didn't ask. I didn't know how to react. She said it so casually. I thought at the time that if she needed help she would ask for it. Now that I'm on the other side, I regret that I hadn't known what to say or how to help.

Once we were young girls getting by; now we've each

crossed a lonely threshold. We are both survivors. I text Melanie about what happened to me and ask her for a call to get advice.

"How are you?" I ask her on the phone.

"I'm okay." Her voice inflects at the end a bit. Not entirely convincing—but how else are we supposed to answer the question, without breaking a dam of pain we are trying to hold inside? I know the feeling.

"How are you?" she asks.

"I'm . . ." I trail off. "I'm sorry, Melanie. For what happened to you."

"I'm sorry, too," Melanie says back.

The statistic of one in four college women rings in my head. Her voice is steady with empathy and understanding, and she continues. "Hey, if you ever need anything, I'm here for you. I know other survivors, too. Others . . . they don't get it. I had someone the other day ask me if I was drinking when it happened."

"Yeah, same."

"I heard that your rapist was from the ███████ final club. Mine was, too."

I feel like she is someone who will understand. So I share, "You know he had the audacity to text me after."

"What!" Melanie's voice changes. It's animated. "My rapist texted me, too!"

My heart races, bracing to hear what else Melanie has to say.

"Something about him not meaning to hurt me, and—"

". . . and wanting to meet up?" we say at the same time.

"Oh my god. That's the same message."

"Word for word."

We sit in disbelief at the realization.

"Do they have some kind of script at the ▇▇▇▇▇ after their members rape girls?"

"I don't know. I wonder if the other women he raped also got the same message. You know several other women came forward against him? Diane needs to know about this . . ."

"Who?" I ask.

"Diane Rosenfeld—she teaches gender-based violence at Harvard Law. She's been secretly helping survivors on campus organize. She's written several laws protecting domestic violence survivors. I can introduce you to her."

•   •   •

The first time I meet Diane, I am terrified. Wasserstein Hall is the jewel of the law school campus, a modern building with large travertine arches. In one wing is the Caspersen Student Center, full of study spaces and lounges. Another wing is home to clinics and classrooms. According to the Harvard website, the building was designed to be "a vibrant crossroads and collaborative environment." In other words, it was designed for people to run into one another—a place where ideas and collaborations could take root organically. That's wonderful for students. Except this time, I am returning to campus not as a student but as a victim. Not an alumna, but a client of one of the clinics in Wasserstein. It does not help my anxiety that clients of the clinics are forbidden from entering the student spaces. There is a separate set of elevators for clients—for victims. It makes me feel like a second-class citizen, despite the good intentions. I want to say, *I went here, too!* I'm afraid of people seeing me enter from the side and wondering why. I feel like a mistress. Like I have done something wrong.

I rapidly press the button over and over again to call the elevator, knowing it will not speed anything up. But it keeps my mind occupied from the embarrassment and shame I feel standing on the Harvard Law campus as a victim of the law, a survivor in need of help. Once the doors finally open, I dash inside and confine myself to a corner. The doors take eons to close.

The elevator opens to the lobby. But there is still a door with an ID lock blocking the entrance to the violence against women clinic. I hug the big teal folder of materials close to my chest. A person at the front desk sees me through the glass doors. The door buzzes and I enter. In the waiting room, I wonder if this front desk person knows why I am here. Does she know I was raped? Does everyone in this clinic know? As I start to seek more help, I realize I can no longer control who knows and who doesn't know this painful, personal part of who I am. I cannot control the stigma, the dirty scarlet letter that will brand me forever. *A rape victim.* And I need to be prepared for others to see me that way for the rest of my life.

"She's ready for you." The front desk attendant snaps me out of my thoughts.

Professor Rosenfeld's office is different from the rest of Harvard's grand, ostentatious architecture. Plants line the ridges of her windows and desk. Soft, plush, quilted cushions lend a sense of comfort. It feels more like a safe space than a clinical lawyer's office. In here, the pain feels manageable. Like there's still a shot for hope.

The office is warm—a reflection of its proprietor. Diane radiates warmth. A thousand-watt smile accompanies her curly blond hair, which surrounds her face like a halo. An angel of the law. She's physically small but a heavyweight in her field. Many students apply to Harvard Law because of her. She is the country's foremost legal scholar on violence against women. The laws she's penned have saved thousands of women. Diane rises out of her desk chair to meet me at her office door. She smiles at me with compassion while leading me to her seating area. I know she's met many survivors like me, right here on these chairs. I wonder how many of them leave this office feeling a greater sense of hope. I wonder how I will leave.

"Professor—"

"You can call me Diane."

I struggle with her kindness.

"Thank you so much for meeting with me today, *Diane*. I don't know if you had the chance to read my email—I wanted to know if it was true."

I open the teal folder and pull out the brochure and motion to the words "At the end of six months, it will be destroyed." She accepts the paper gently, holds it with gravity.

"I did read it. I've had some of my legal policy workshop students look into it, too." She pauses. "It's true, Massachusetts does destroy untested rape kits. And there exist no standard operating procedures to extend the timeline."

My hope drains quickly. Diane cannot help. She can't help because the law won't let her, won't let anyone. I'm holding back a flood of tears. It feels like someone has smashed my face in. I wonder if she can tell just from looking at me.

"I'm sorry our criminal justice system has failed you. I'm so sorry it fails all of us."

The floodgates burst. Both tears and words flow out of me.

"I've been researching rape kits. The more I look, the more I uncover the systemic secrets holding rape victims down. This is bigger than me. There are over a hundred thousand rape victims in Massachusetts. How many thousands of rape victims have had their justice destroyed by the government? There are so many of us, and yet shame and stigma keep us isolated. Keep us from sharing what has happened. We only talk about it in hushed corners. Afraid of the real retribution of being branded a rape victim. How is it that we are punished for the violence that happened to us? How is it that the world has gaslit society into making *us* the pariahs? It's societally and institutionally ingrained into the system—they punish us."

Diane can see how riled up I am. She leans over in her chair, stretches out her arms, and takes my hands into hers.

"Do you know what a bonobo is?" she asks. "Bonobos are one of our most closely related evolutionary cousins. They are living proof that the patriarchy is not inevitable. Bonobos form a female network—when one of their females is hurt, they rush immediately to her defense from wherever they are. That's how they have eliminated male sexual coercion. I will help you. Consider yourself part of the bonobo sisterhood.

Some of my students here at the law school focus on drafting proposals to lawmakers. If you want, you could talk to them about working on this."

I feign a polite smile back at Diane. "I'll think about it."

I am already drowning in our legal system. So, too, are the thousands of victims whose kits are destroyed. We are all drowning in our own private ocean. Can they hear our cries, under the surface? Or do they just not care? Either way, we are powerless.

Unbeknownst to Diane, in my mailbox, I've just received a letter from arguably the most powerful people in the world, congratulating me on advancing to the final stages of the hiring process to join the CIA. The manila envelope holds instructions for my security. How to take a taxi without revealing where I'm going. How to have a "practical and consistent story about the reason for [my] travel that is not affiliated with the United States Government." How to come up with a "fictitious last name if any taxicab service insists on a last name." In my mind, this job could save me from ever having to return to California. Securing a job means securing a future in which I can finally be safe.

The dates for my final interview and testing appointments are April 14–16, 2014. Exactly six months from when I was hospitalized for my rape kit. It's the date I'll need to save my evidence by, the date, by law, when the government will destroy my rape kit. Fate finds a way to converge. When the clock runs out, I'll have to choose: justice or my career.

11.

Siren Sea

The wind whispers through my hair, rushes upward, and makes the sail of the junk dance in the air. It is the only trill in an otherwise silent melody, the sea hushed as if the world has been lulled to sleep. It is as if a lady of the heavens has unfolded a splendid nightgown of a thousand glimmering stars sewn against a velvety fabric of celestial, infinite vastness. The Milky Way twirls across it, arcing through the night sky. Beneath us, a wonder just as exquisite boldly competes with the stars: the smooth-as-glass sea that our ship glides across. For as far as our eyes can see, in all four cardinal directions, thousands of stars are mirrored. The reflection is broken only by the glow of blue bioluminescence, where the water grazes our ship. Occasionally, schools of fish announce themselves with their phosphorescence, creating an underwater light show.

Crisp salt air fills my lungs with each breath I take. 5 is resting in my arms. The vines of poison have started to creep up her neck. I have been tasked with taking care of her while 15 and 22 are on the bridge, making sense of the compass and steering the wheel in accordance with it. The moon drips liquid silver on everything it touches. On my skin, the glow feels like an embrace.

15 comes down from the bridge. The moonshine creates a silver halo radiating from her hair.

"I didn't know something as beautiful as this could exist."

"The night sky is a place that's strange and splendid, but we forget it exists for us every night," I tell her. "Most of us just don't remember to look up and see it. I always feel better when I do. Those photons have traveled millions of years to reach our eyes. We are able to be cognizant. To understand our existence. To feel, to love—and yet we are but a blink of an eye in the universe. It makes me feel so humbled and special at the same time."

"30, can I ask you something?" 15 pauses as if to build up courage. "Do I ever feel pretty?"

I smile at the question. "15, I remember being you. You worry that you're not skinny enough, not beautiful enough, but as you experience the privilege of aging, you'll look back on yourself with kind eyes. With compassion. With disbelief, even—how could I ever think I was anything but pretty? In fact, you are beautiful. More than that, you are *enough*."

15 lunges at me—surprise hug. She sandwiches 5 in between us.

"Let's hug 22, too. She needs it."

"That's a great idea, 15."

We sneak up—5 grabs 22's legs, 15 tackles her shoulders. We all tumble to the floor, laughing. My arm swings over 22's shoulder, 15 holds 5's hand, and together we gaze in silence at the majesty of the moon. We could stay in this moment for an eternity.

. . .

We take shifts at the helm so that each of us gets some sleep. 15 is on the bridge now, while 22 and 5 are sleeping. I join 15.

"Do you know what constellation that is?" I ask her.

"Orion?"

"Yes! I know he's a hunter, but he looks like he's dancing to me."

"You think we'll ever make it? Touch the stars?"

"As an astronaut? We're trying to. I spent my twenties surviving. Surviving brought me to places far and wide— the halls of Congress, the United Nations, around the globe. But my activism came at a steep personal cost to my actual dreams.

"When I started my activism, I made a promise to myself. That one day, when I passed the law, I would return. I didn't need to sacrifice my dreams to do good. Life is about choices. Many people become activists because life threw them a storm and they chose to rage back. But the stars have never been out of sight, still always twinkling above.

"I want all survivors to know that not only can we survive

and change the world, but also we do not need to give up what we love. I've started training part-time in astronautics research as a route to finding a way back home to the stars."

"I'm glad I could meet you, 30."

"Me, too. I wish I could reach back in time and tell you this in real life, 15."

"I hear it still, 30. I am still inside you."

As I smile, I look back at where I left 22 and 5. I wish 22 could hear this, too. I still remember her pain, her rage. 5 is peering over at the water.

"Hey! 5! Remember what Bargaining warned us about," I shout at her. "We shouldn't look at the water too long! They're fake memories, and they're dangerous!"

But she's transfixed, unmoving. I run and grab her, jolting 5 back to the present. Her little hands have started climbing over the boat, and she's hanging from her waist now, head over the ledge. She's squirming out of my grip.

"It's Mom! And Dad!" 5 squeals. My heart races.

"They're not really here! It's not real!" 15 shouts.

"Yes it is!" 5 retorts.

"Hold her back, 30," 22 insists.

I grip my arms around 5 even tighter. Rain has started to fall, loosening my hold.

"Maybe this can help me," 5 says. "I know it! I already feel better!"

The wind has started to pick up. We're sailing at full speed. The helm has started to turn.

"Help me!" 15 begs as she leans her full weight on the

wheel to keep it from spinning. 22 runs to hold the wheel down.

Waves are starting to form, bouncing us as 5 reaches farther toward the glowing water. I follow my line of sight along her hand and grip it back. I see what she sees. It's Mom laughing while pressing wonton wrappers together to make dumplings. Dad is cooking breakfast. 5 is setting the table. He's drawn happy faces with the sriracha sauce. Mom hands him a piece of lettuce. He chomps on it: "Look, I'm a dinosaur!" We are happy.

I gasp. The memory itself isn't true, but it's an amalgamation of pieces of true joyful memories, forged into one. I know this isn't real. They're not there in the water. But the glowing water looks like a portal. Like I could just jump right in and be there, live in that false memory, the rare and only happy moments we've all locked away because they are too painful to remember. It's difficult to think that the people who hurt us aren't only monsters, that they are humans. How is it possible to reconcile their violence while also loving them?

I snap out of my thoughts too late.

A wave splashes onto the deck, and 5 jumps off. She is gone. Just as soon, the sea erupts into a tidal storm. 22 and 15 are panicked. They are screaming at me, but I can't hear what they are saying. I knew I could have held 5 back, but the truth is I felt the water on me as she splashed. I felt what it felt like to have a happy mom and dad. And the reality is I let her jump. Deep down I wanted that memory, too.

"SNAP OUT OF IT!" 22 screams as she shakes me. But

time has slowed, drugged by the memory I saw. She grabs a life preserver, tugs the rope to make sure that it's secured to the boat, and ties the other end of the rope around her waist.

The rain is pouring heavily. There are no more visible stars. Darkness envelops all. The wind howls as the ship lurches against the waves. Only yelling can cut through the noise.

"I'm going in after 5!" 22 places a part of the rope in my hands. "When I shoot the red flare, pull us back in."

She dives, without hesitation, into the void.

The grogginess has partially lifted from my mind when I see 15's face, terrified. She's done a hell of a job holding down the wheel. I have failed to do mine. I look in the direction of 22 and 5.

BANG!

A red flare flashes through the rain. Thank god.

I brace my right leg against the ship and begin pulling with all my strength. Lightning lights up the sky. I see a flash of figures at the end of the rope. I pull and pull and pull. I haul as hard as I can and yank up the life preserver. There's only one person holding on to it—it's 5.

12.

TIME LOOP

It's April 1, 2014. I have fourteen days left until my kit is destroyed—20,160 minutes, and each one stings me as it passes. Staring at the clock, I watch the second hand glide across its orbit. Another minute down. Every tick brings me closer to the end.

I'm sitting in my home in Washington, DC. "Where all roads lead if you want to change the world!" I remember with a sigh. Changing the world feels impossible when I can't even change my own. My 548-square-foot studio apartment in Chinatown overlooks a grimy alleyway full of dumpsters. It sits directly across from government housing. The studio is on the fourth floor of a fourteen-floor apartment complex—too low to see the sky, but low enough to hear the voices of back-alley arguments ricochet against the narrow, stacked buildings on our row. Looking out this window is claustrophobic. The blinds are cheap plastic that snaps at the slightest touch and fails at its only job in the world, which is blocking out the harsh, unwelcome light of the world outside. I do my best to make the inside homey. A thrifted $10 yellow wingback chair from Craigslist brightens up a corner. On it, a stuffed plushie the shape of a space shuttle sits. I hang up retro NASA posters that depict what life would be like on different exoplanets. A wooden dining table—salvaged from a couple moving out who were ready to throw it away—takes up the heart of the room. There is no space for a couch. In the corner, my IKEA work desk and bed are squished together. On the desk, my "Never Never Never Give Up" sign rests, still taped to the monitor that hooks up to my laptop. Birthday cards from my Boston friends are taped to the walls as makeshift decoration. It's the first place I can truly call my own.

The truth is that transitioning from Boston to DC has been hard. A happy hour Harvard threw for recent graduates felt like torture. I lasted for only fifteen minutes before leaving. Every conversation began with "What do you do?"—DC's most clichéd code phrase, a shorthand inquiry people use to size you up and deem if you are worthy of their time.

"I'm in the onboarding process of the CIA, training to become a spy. How about you?" Nope—can't say that. So I try my best to deflect. If you're lucky enough to clear the first line of questioning, people will ask you about your hobbies and pastimes in the city. "My hobby is tracking down forensic labs to save my rape kit from destruction—because oh, by the way, did I mention I was raped recently?" Turns out it isn't the greatest icebreaker. No matter. The thought of making new friends or ingratiating myself to strangers seems pointless at the moment, anyway. I cannot talk about my job process at the CIA. And I cannot talk about what preoccupies every waking moment of my life, which is my mission to save my evidence. My truth feels so secretive, so shameful, so far from a normal twentysomething's life that I opt out of being around people entirely. It feels too hard to keep putting on a fake persona of normality when my world is crumbling apart. My social battery is fried. I self-isolate completely.

Fourteen days left until my kit is destroyed. I look at the paperwork the CIA has sent me. Thirteen days from now, on April 14, my final round of tests will include:

An aptitude test

A one-on-one interview (three to four hours long)

A group interview

A psychological assessment and evaluation

I glance at my computer, straining to allocate its memory under the weight of a hundred open tabs. I know how it feels. The tabs mirror the jumbled, urgent thoughts now straining for attention within my mind. "Analysis of Putin." "Soft Power." "Massachusetts Justice Department." I genuinely want to serve in the CIA. In my application, I had written, "Home is where I first learned to respect the freedoms I have been given in this country. I grew up listening to my family members' stories of service and the price they paid to gain the freedoms that I was born with. I want to serve my country. I am motivated to give back. At the end of the day, I think that the agency is made up of people who want to serve and strongly believe in the freedoms that this country stands for."

But increasingly, I feel torn between the ideals that I hold for America and the reality of what it is like to live in it. On paper, I still remain motivated by the chance that I could bring about some change in the world—that I could spur the government into action by becoming a small part of it. But with each dead end and disappointment after my rape, each failure and frustration, that chance grows slimmer in my mind.

Saving my kit is about more than preserving my evidence—I also need it taken care of so I can focus on these tests and move forward with my future. Every step to save the kit continues to be a battle. Even the simplest interactions, like talking to the rape crisis center, have proven difficult. The center makes it a point to not converse over email, because emails can be hacked; as a result, everything has to be done over the phone. That means playing phone tag, sporadic access to information, inconsistent communication with whoever happens to be there on any given day, and having to talk through incredibly sensitive information in detail, over and over again. These frustrations may sound relatively minor given everything else a survivor endures, but they pile up, day after day, contributing to the heap of secondary traumatization that you go through simply hunting for clues about what to do next.

For weeks I have reached out to lawyers, the Harvard police, and the rape crisis center to better understand what it would take to get an extension on my rape kit. It's all come up short. A couple days ago, I called the rape crisis center over and over until I was finally able to talk to someone. The staffer said they had connections with the forensic lab where my rape kit was held and would contact them to find out if the kit could be extended—but of course, they would not confirm that via email. They'd call me back, they said.

I sleep with my phone next to me, waiting. Waiting to hear whether my evidence has been destroyed. Whether my rape mattered. Whether I matter. As the date nears, I become more and more distressed. I feel like I'm slowly going crazy. I count the minutes. I feel like a lamb headed to slaughter. I can see the slaughterhouse—but no matter how hard I scream, the belt of time keeps moving me closer and closer and closer to the moment when my opportunity for justice will be destroyed.

My phone rings. It's the rape crisis center.

"The kit has been extended," the staffer tells me.

"THANK GOD!" I exclaim. "As you can understand, this is extremely important to me being able to pursue justice. Can I please get an email confirmation that the rape kit has been extended, so I can have written proof?"

"No, I'm sorry, it's against our policy to do that."

"But how am I supposed to have any hard evidence for this?" I ask. "I'm in DC. What if I fly to Boston? You can't email me, but can you print out your email exchange and hand me the hard copy?"

"We can do that."

I don't understand the logic of this, but I am not going to question it. I will fly 439 miles to get a printout of an email they could have forwarded to me with one click. Why do survivors have to jump through these ridiculous hoops in order to save our own evidence? I spend $538 on a round-trip flight to go to the rape crisis center in Massachusetts and pick up the printed-out confirmation, then will fly back to Washington just in time for the world's most intense job interview. What about survivors who don't have $500 to burn? Do they never receive hard proof that their kit has been extended or even destroyed? Everything is difficult, inaccessible, impossible. It's almost as if the *point* is to stack the criminal justice system against us.

I arrive at the rape crisis center, where I've just spent hundreds of dollars to pick up two pieces of paper. I read the contents.

April 2, 2014

From: Marissa ██████████████ [mailto: ████████████████████████]

Sent: Wednesday, April 2, 2014 9:49 AM

To: ████████, Rachel

Subject: Extension of Kit #██████

Hi Rachel,

The client for kit number ██████ contacted us at BARCC asking for her kit to be extended. She still has not decided if she would like to report the incident to the police or not but the six month timeframe is coming up. Please let me know if there is anything else I can do.

Thanks,
Marissa

From: ████████, Rachel (POL)
Sent: Wednesday, April 2, 2014 10:42 AM
To: Marissa ████████████████
Subject: Extension of Kit #██████

Hi Marissa,

We do have that kit here. For future reference, our lab case # is ████████. I will make the request to extend the storage here for another six months.

Rachel

The final approval email is a message that is just four simple words. "Request done and accepted." Three simple emails. It's surreal to look at those words in their cold simplicity—such a nonchalant exchange, papering over the impossible weight of what it truly means.

There's that tug-of-war again. On the one hand, I'm relieved that my kit has been saved, at least for now. On the other, I'm enraged that every part of this process is like pulling teeth, every step a hassle, every rule another absurd artificial barrier to my peace of mind. Relief wins out for the moment: my kit is safe. The door to justice is still open to me, and I can focus on preparing for my career.

As I walk down the streets of Cambridge, that short-lived relief gives way to a realization. In a flash of horror, it dawns on me: I haven't stopped the clock. I've only reset it.

Every six months, I'll have to relive this nightmare and re-trace the steps of this second betrayal, pleading once again for another reprieve. With no standard procedure for extending my kit, I've entered into yet another loop, a Sisyphean purgatory created just for survivors. A six-month cycle of requests and extensions, of needless flights and holding my breath, of organizing my life in an orbit around the day that I was raped. The justice system has sentenced me to live like this until I decide, forever cognizant of the day of my rape, marking heinous anniversaries again and again. The system will not let me ignore it; if I ever slip and forget to observe even one of my rape kit's god-awful birthdays or half-birthdays, I'll lose my chance at justice forever.

This is an atrocity designed to punish survivors, to dis-suade us from wanting to seek justice. To pummel the thought out of us. I am stuck in their spin cycle, reliving the system's betrayal over and over and over and over again.

TIME REMAINING UNTIL EVIDENCE DESTRUCTION: 14 DAYS

It's September 30, 2014. I have two weeks left in my second loop—20,160 minutes until my kit is destroyed. Once again, I watch the small hand of the clock glide across its orbit. Once again, another minute ticks away.

I'm sitting in my home in Washington, DC. "Where all roads lead if you want to change the world!" But my road is a cul-de-sac, like the one I grew up on—a cul-de-sac like the one I once thought I'd escaped. I loop around again, right back where I was.

Maybe this time will be different—after all, I've got a ticket in my hand to escape my parents. It's an acceptance letter from the CIA. Could this be the key that finally breaks that loop?

The government is notorious for taking a long time to do anything. The CIA proves to be the same. I received my acceptance letter a month after my interviews, but still, five months later, more tests remain before I can actually begin. It really is the world's toughest onboarding process.

In the meantime, it feels like I am treading water, barely able to survive and drained of energy. When I try to gulp in air, I inhale a rush of water. All of my time feels sucked up by survival: taking pains to land a stable job and desperately trying to track down and protect my evidence. I feel as though if I stop for even a second—if I allow myself to stop treading water—I will drown.

In the back of my mind, Diane's offer to help me draft up a new policy with her Harvard Law students glows like a small ember. I don't have time to give it the oxygen it needs to grow into a fire—but I can feel that the heat is there. The truth is that I don't see myself as an activist. I'm not like Charlize. She's bold and daring and doesn't care what people think. But I do—I care very much. I care what the CIA thinks about me. I care what the White House thinks. Most of all, I care how NASA sees me. All places that have rigid standards for their candidates; all places that are risk averse by nature. All three will make candidates list any ongoing legal cases they're involved with. If I make the choice to officially file my rape with the police, it will absolutely be taken into consideration by the institutions I one day hope to serve. At every turn, I see another roadblock, another demerit, another strike against survivors thrown up by the world. I see, in real time, how the violence that is brought upon us can be held against us socially and professionally. Now I understand why Charlize was so passionate about advocating for survivors' rights on campus.

Even though I suppressed any mention of the rape in my interview, the assault and its aftermath came up in the CIA's psych evaluation.

The evaluation took place in an undisclosed CIA building—a nondescript office space. Not like those creepy, dimly lit, two-way interrogation rooms I'd endured during previous tests. There was a snake plant in the corner by the windowsill. How cheery. It was a hair past noon. The summer sun shined brightly through the windows, so hot that I felt like I could still get sunburned from the inside.

"You tested to be resistant against authority," the psychologist evaluator said. She must have been in her seventies, but I swear she was in her nineties. Maybe over a hundred? I don't know what they're capable of in the CIA. She reminded me of the old line about the agency—that it's harder to get out than it is to get in—and as I compared the snow-white hair of my interrogator to the young brunette smiling at me from the photo on the badge strung around her neck, I sensed the truth of that expression.

Tap tap tap. She flicked a pen in between her index finger and the table. This was not helping my anxiety. She swiveled on her desk chair, grabbed a massive binder, and dropped it on the table that divided us with a resounding *THUD.* Pressing her thin-rimmed gold glasses up the bridge of her nose, the evaluator squinted as she flipped through the leviathan. This textbook of me was clearly put together by all those creepy people behind the two-way interrogation rooms I'd entered before.

"What do you make of that?"

"I speak my mind," I told her.

Back in my apartment, I reflect on my choice to not speak up publicly and in my job interviews about this nightmare. I have fought back, but only within a narrow set of parameters, only in the context of my immediate needs. I am merely trying to preserve my own kit, not make a big fuss about how backward this system is. The truth all along is that I have not spoken my mind because it would risk my career. If I allowed myself to speak, I'd scream at the police, at the rape crisis center, at whichever politicians created this six-month rule.

The ember of Diane's offer to rewrite the law is starting to glow stronger. There must be a better way to extend the kit than playing phone tag with the crisis center and spending hundreds of dollars to fly back to Massachusetts to beg for proof of my evidence being preserved. I decide to finally email Diane to ask for help.

September 30, 2014

Hi Diane!

It's been a couple months since I checked in—I was hospitalized October 14, a date that is coming up soon. To my understanding, every 6 months I have to extend my rape kit. Do you have any guidance for this? Is there a more direct way to do this than through the Boston Area Rape Crisis Center? Communication with them is so difficult. I understand that for privacy reasons they don't communicate via email, but that makes it so much harder for me to have written proof and solid confirmation/evidence. Any advice would be appreciated.

True to her bonobo sisterhood values, Diane offers to contact the rape crisis center to follow up. Hopefully, her position as a lawyer at Harvard will help elicit a quicker response. She doesn't hear back from them.

Over the next few days, as my countdown clock dwindles away, I call the Cambridge Police Department. They tell me that because I was raped on Harvard's campus, they can't help me—my case is with the Harvard University Police Department. When I call Harvard's police department, they say *they* can't help me—it's Cambridge's jurisdiction, since I was admitted to Brigham and Women's Hospital. I am getting bounced back and forth like a ball.

TIME REMAINING UNTIL EVIDENCE DESTRUCTION:
12 DAYS

Thursday, October 2

The Harvard police and the rape crisis center tell me two conflicting pieces of information. The police tell me that my kit is being held at the Cambridge Police Property & Evidence Unit "indefinitely"—but a rare email exchange with the rape crisis center clearly states that my kit is at the state lab, where survivors have to renew it every six months. That means one of them is wrong, and it feels to me like one of them is lying. I try desperately over the next several days to reach out to my former bosses, lawyers, nonprofits, anyone who could be helpful. My emails read:

> I was admitted to Brigham hospital on October 14, 2013. My
> kit number is ▮▮▮▮▮ and it was brought to the State Police
> Lab by The Cambridge Police Department (Case Number
> ▮▮▮▮▮▮▮). I cannot find anyone who can help me extend
> the kit. Neither the state lab line nor the Boston area rape crisis
> center (BARCC). I don't know what to do. This rape kit has my
> medical evidence in it. It is my access to justice in the future.
> I'm so scared of losing it. I don't want it to be destroyed. I
> don't know what to do. Please help me.

Some respond, but none of them can offer a solution.

TIME REMAINING UNTIL EVIDENCE DESTRUCTION:
4 DAYS

Friday, October 10
I spend my birthday sobbing. My world is spinning off its axis.

TIME REMAINING UNTIL EVIDENCE DESTRUCTION:
3 DAYS

Saturday, October 11
Cambridge police state they do not have it. Harvard police state they do not have it. No one knows where my kit is. Has it already been destroyed? It seems impossible—the deadline won't be reached for three more days—but then again, anything seems possible in the cruel confines of this system. I've called the crisis center continually, but because they are chronically understaffed, I do not hear back from them. Then I remember the paper trail. I rush to find the printout of the email exchange I'd picked up in Boston six months earlier. The date the kit was extended wasn't April 14, the day it was set to be destroyed. It was April 2, which means my countdown might be off by twelve days. Oh fuck—what if I've already missed the deadline? What if my kit has already been destroyed?

Clutching my chest, I scream into my pillow. My lungs are on fire, burning with the betrayal of those who were supposed to help me through this. I am begging to be heard. Pleading for the bare minimum from a country that promised me I would be treated with dignity if I was a good survivor. If I went to the hospital; if I went to the police. There is no such thing as a good survivor, I now know, only an inconvenient one who must be beaten into submission by a system that simply doesn't care.

Everything I had worked for feels as though it has slipped out of my grasp once again. All the research, the meetings with Diane, the cold calls with the forensic labs, the hours of sobbing, of praying—all gone. The hours in the hospital—gone. My justice—gone. This is not worth it. The whiplash is searing.

I'd never known a pain like this. A pain so deep that it preys on your soul. A pain that makes you want to sever your tongue. In that moment, I am ready to drown.

What keeps me afloat, if only barely, is the knowledge that my death would let them win—not only my rapist, but the system that permits him to go on breathing freely while survivors like me gasp for air. I cannot abide the idea. So while I know that I will never be the person I was before I was raped—and I will never be the person I was before my own government tossed me into the machine and put me through the ringer—I cannot die before they hear from me.

Through my tears, I notice a detail on my printed confirmation that I hadn't seen before: the direct email of the state lab technician.

If the crisis center won't respond to me, I'll email the lab tech directly.

October 11, 2014

Hi Rachel,

In April you extended my rape kit, the kit number itself is ▓▓▓▓ and the lab case is # ▓▓▓▓▓▓▓, for another

6 months. I have scanned in a copy of the email between you and the BARCC representative that asked for your extension. I would like to extend my kit and preserve my access to justice. Any information or guidance would be helpful.

CC'd are my attorneys.

Thank you.

Sincerely,
Amanda

I get an email instantly back. My heart skips a beat.

Subject: Out of Office: Rape Kit Extension #████████

I will be out of the office until 4/13/15. Please contact Gloria ████████ during my absence.

Until April? Oh my god. I reach out to Diane for help.

Hi Diane,

I did some digging around and found the printed email that I demanded BARCC give me—turns out it is very helpful! On the email it has the name and contact of the state lab technical leader who extended my kit. The problems are that 1) she doesn't work there anymore and 2) It seems like they extended it from April 2 so it's past 6 months.

TIME LOOP

I would like to find out where exactly my kit is, extend it, and understand what the best way to extend it in the future is.

Could we, at your earliest convenience, call the state lab and CPD's property and evidence unit (contact below)? I need someone, namely an advocate like you to help me be firm with the Cambridge Police. I'm getting bounced back and forth like a ball. I know for a fact that my kit is not at HUPD. More information and leads can't hurt!

On the plate:

1) Call CPD's Property Evidence Unit to verify if in fact my kit is there

2) Call Gloria

3) Wait to hear back from the message you left with CPD's Sgt

4) Wait to hear back from HUPD's Detective about clarification of kit status

5) Wait to hear back from the Middlesex District Attorney's office

Again thank you to you both for helping through this. I so greatly appreciate it.

Amanda

DAY OF DESTRUCTION

October 14

Diane and I call whomever we can, and finally we get through to Gloria. Diane, Gloria, and I have a brief conversation. She's cold and seems like she can't be bothered to understand what I've had to go through to get to her. Even so, I take comfort in the fact that there finally seems to be a way to save my kit. After our conversation, I write to Gloria to express how much saving my evidence means to me.

October 14, 2014

Hi Gloria,

Thank you so much for calling me today. Per our discussion, I am following up on our talk about extending my rape kit, #███████, service date 10/14/13, lab case #███████████, to the full extent of how long kits can be extended, which—to my knowledge—is max 6 months at a time.

Gloria, I cannot emphasize enough what a difference your call today made in my life. As a rape survivor, access to my medical evidence—and thus possible justice—is a huge deal. Even if the current system sets up obstacles, what you did today by simply telling me how to extend my kit broke down a barrier. If I can process this kit, it would only empower me to have more information, and make better decisions. In this storm, knowing what my options are—information—is everything. Knowledge is power.

You lifted me out of darkness and for that, in as deeply as electronic ink can express it, thank you.

Hopeful,
Amanda

The reply:

October 15, 2014

Hello,

I have forwarded your request to my supervisor for more guidance on how to proceed with an examination request. In the meantime, I put a note in our system to preserve the kit for six more months and I also alerted the evidence unit supervisors so they are aware of the request.

Gloria
Acting Technical Leader—Criminalistics and Crime Scene Response

Gloria doesn't even address me by my name—to her, I'm a number, a case file, another anonymous victim, as distant as an exoplanet. On my exoplanet, I am constantly dodging fireballs, struggling to survive without a moment to breathe. In their world, everything is clinical and depersonalized. I've now had countless interactions in which I find myself pleading with professionals to have some empathy, to understand why I am fighting to save my evidence. At every turn I feel like I have to convince people of the obvious and get them to care—*hi! I was raped. Being raped is considered bad. The government systematically destroys critical rape evidence. I think that's bad. Please don't destroy my evidence. It doesn't help me. It doesn't help law enforcement. It does not help anyone to destroy evidence. Please understand why this is CRAZY!*

I feel like I am being gaslighted by every interaction I have with a person representing our justice system. Perhaps it's clinical detachment. Perhaps they work with so many rape victims it just doesn't impact them anymore. Oh! Another girl raped. One in four. Just another day on the job. I later learn that what I am experiencing is called the lack of trauma-informed service. To top off the insult, the police get back to me after the destruction deadline of my kit with wrong information about where the kit was.

Something inside me breaks. I can't keep doing this. I can't live my life going hysterical every six months. Something has to change—and I know more than ever that I have to change it.

I have to change the system, come hell or high water. I will break this time loop. I will escape. Even if it means I have to rewrite the law.

I spend the next few days putting my thoughts together in an email. I copy nearly everyone I know.

November 1, 2014

Friends, Survivors, Teammates, and Allies:

This campaign's objective is to establish a Bill of Rights for the Sexual Assault Survivors of Massachusetts. My drive to create this bill stems from my treatment by the police, who continually misinformed me about the status of my rape kit. Had I believed them and not made my own inquiries, my medical evidence would have been wrongfully destroyed.

I've always had great faith in and respect for our law enforcement. Even though local law enforcement has failed me, what happened to me does not diminish their mission to serve. This campaign is focused on raising voices, clarifying the needs of survivors and clearly establishing what protocols and rights survivors are entitled to. We continually wrestle with how to reconcile the demands of a broken system meant to administer justice with the needs of those the system is meant to serve. The status quo fails to live up to our ideals. Let's change that.

This past week, I met with survivors, coalitions, allies to talk about this campaign. The outpour of survivors sharing their stories has been truly moving. There is momentum here and I'm excited to have your support. This email list will serve as a weekly update to the movement. The list includes our legal team comprised of Harvard Law professor Diane Rosenfeld and Harvard Law students assisting with the drafting of the bill. It includes the organizing team, comprised of different key stakeholders across MA. Lastly, it includes advisers from different coalitions and other allies from across the US who are professionals in this field. Thank you all for your support.

Rape inherently disempowers. In a twist of irony, survivors have the most powerful voice to contribute to this movement. I wish I could talk to every survivor and tell them that your bravery and your struggles are heard. I am here to hear them. I know your anguish. I share it. And that's why it is ever so important at this moment to rally together and push for a better future. This system is accountable to us. We have the power to make a difference.

For too long I stayed silent, scared by rape culture. I could no longer stay quiet. Silence is not an option. I am no longer afraid because I know I am not alone. But I cannot do this without each and every one of you that is on this list. Let's show the rest of the nation that Massachusetts can be at the forefront of this change that is sweeping the nation. The time is now. The time is now to protect the rights of those who need them the most.

I walk towards the future, cognizant that this campaign won't be easy. More importantly, I walk towards the future filled with profound, extraordinary hope.

Walk with me.
Amanda

I am speaking up now. The fire is roaring.

13.

The Lighthouse Keeper

Where is 22!" 15 screams from the helm.

5, still dazed, clothes soaking wet and sputtering water out of her mouth, doesn't answer. Although she is back on the boat, 5 clutches the life preserver with white-knuckled fear. The waves and wind have settled, but the storm still rages above. Rain pours from the sky. Lightning flashes. I rush to comfort 5.

"Where is 22?" I ask her, trying to be gentle.

5 starts crying, rocking back and forth. Her little lips quiver. "I'm sorry. I'm sorry."

"It's okay. Just tell me what happened," I insist.

"She's gone. She was with me on the life preserver, and then a wave came and she was gone."

"IT WAS YOUR FUCKING JOB TO HOLD HER, THIRTY!" 15 explodes. Thunder roars behind her. 5 drops the life preserver and dives into my arms, shivering. I hold 5 close.

"We have to go back and find her!" 15 shrieks.

"We don't have time." I point to 5's arms, which have turned solidly purple. "What could we do? The storm is still going; we're just as likely to get pulled down by the water. The keepers of the realms would know what to do. Bargaining would know what to do. He's the one who told us the rules. We must be close to Sadness. They'll know what to do."

"You had one job! You couldn't even do it! You're going to let 22 drown? Let your own self drown?! How could you betray yourself!"

"I'm sorry, 15. I'm sorry I failed to protect 5. I'm sorry I failed to protect 22."

A lightning strike illuminates 15, forming a different type of halo. This is the first time I've seen her like this. This is the first time 15 has broken her perfect persona, her veneer of teenage deference and docility finally giving way to defiance. As it breaks through, she begins to look like 22.

"Look!" 5 points through the fog. In the distance, a lighthouse shines. "That must be Sadness's light."

We moor our boat on the sand and jump off it as soon as we can. I'm carrying 5 on my hip and dashing toward the door of the lighthouse.

The tower is enormous. It rises about thirty stories high. Even in the storm, I can make out alternating colored stripes painted around the lighthouse. At the top, a beacon swirls, creating a cone of brightness that rotates completely on the minute.

15 pounds on the wooden door. The hinges creak as the door opens; warmth pours out. A small elderly lady appears. Her gray hair, held up in a bun, shines against the orange glow of a fireplace behind her. She wears a quilted apron covered in white stars on a black background.

She smiles. "I'm glad you've found me. Come on in."

I shudder at the transition of temperature. The door closes behind us. Although huge from the outside, the inside of the lighthouse is quaint and cozy. To the left, there is a large tiled kitchen with dozens of dried flowers hanging from the ceiling. Pots, pans, ceramic mugs, and mismatched, delicate porcelain teacups line wooden cabinets. Glass vials containing a rainbow of loose tea leaves sit next to the stove. I spot chamomile yellow, lavender purple, blush pink rose petals, and green jasmine. To the right of the room, a fire roars. Shaggy rugs cover the floors. The smell of fresh baked goods wafts from the oven. The stove is on; a teapot is perched over a flickering burner. Books line the rest of the walls, the shelves filled and practically swirling up the spiraling staircase, out of sight. It looks like an endless library reaching all the way to the top.

"Oh my, you're all soaking wet! Please sit by the fire and grab a blanket," she offers. We oblige.

I curl up in a wingback chair. I take my shoes off and dig my toes into the woolly rug warmed by the fire.

5 grabs a blanket to dry off the storm water from her hair.

"Are you Sadness? We need help. The storm has taken one of us," 15 says, still standing by the door.

"Ah, one of you looked too closely now, huh?

"I can tell you are worried, but don't worry, she isn't gone.

The sea doesn't work like that. Sail back to Bargaining. He'll know how you can find 22." She pauses as she hovers over a teapot on the stovetop. "And yes, I am Sadness. Welcome to my home."

"What did you see?" 15 breathlessly asks me and 5, her hair still dripping wet from the storm. We stand in silence, avoiding eye contact. The water dripping from our hair punctures the quiet.

"WHAT DID YOU SEE?" she screams at us.

5 murmurs, her mind still in the memory, "Mom and Dad . . ."

". . . being happy," I say, completing her sentence.

15's face contorts from anger into heartache.

Sadness speaks through our miserable sobs. "Your saddest memories aren't of pain," she explains. "They're of grief, the potential of happiness that cannot be."

The kettle whistles, puffs of white steam rising from its nozzle. Sadness moves it from the stovetop and pours the contents into three teacups. The tea looks like golden honey, bouncing light from the fireplace as the steam floats.

"Here's something that'll help warm you from the inside as well." Sadness extends her hand. I take the tea, enjoying the heat seeping into my fingers. The scent of jasmine wafts up in my face, the steam spreading. I breathe in deeply and take a sip. The warmth glides on my tongue and slides down my throat. It feels like a hug from the inside. Then I see the porcelain teacup has cursive letters on the outside.

"Humanity? What's in this cup?" I ask, confused.

"Humanity," Sadness states matter-of-factly.

"I thought you were Sadness. What gift does Sadness impart?" 15 asks.

Sadness answers with a smile. "If you find me, you're on the right track. Not numb from denial, not blind from anger, not bargaining out of delusion. Sadness is an integral part of the human condition. All of us must experience it. For without it, life is meaningless. Sadness is a lighthouse that guides you in the storm to tell you about the love you have for what and who truly matter to you. Every cup tastes different based on the person drinking it."

"I taste cereal milk!" 5 exclaims.

"Mine tastes like Mother's phở," 15 mumbles.

I sip my cup again. "Jasmine, like the tea I used to drink at Harvard."

"What's with all the books?" 15 asks.

"They're your stories. Not only the ones you've lived, but also the ones you've been told."

I look at the titles more clearly. They are marked by day, month, and year. On the first shelf a book title reads, *October 10, 1991*.

"Is this . . . a collection of our life?" I ponder out loud.

"Yes, this lighthouse is a library of your memories—every floor corresponds to a year that you've lived. Thirty floors for thirty years of life."

"Wait, I can read about my future in detail?" 15 questions.

"No, unfortunately only 30 may go to all floors. Every year of life means the lighthouse grows a little taller."

I place my teacup down and touch the spines of the books.

"Thank you, Sadness. I could spend a lifetime lost in

reading these memories. But 5 is sick, and we need to get to the next realm. Can you tell us how?"

"Tell me the saddest story you know."

5 gets up from the fire and walks over to the first shelf. She pulls a story out labeled "Lan, 1978" and hands it to Sadness.

"This one! Mom's story. Can you read it for us?"

Sadness brings it back near the fireplace, sits on a chair, opens the book, and begins reading it. A bright light emanates from its pages and pulls us into the story.

•   •   •

Death is a symphony.

It was to the twenty-nine people fleeing on the wooden boat. Wind whipping, bullets whistling, death raining, planting souls left to be harvested by Hades. To return them to the abyss. The pitch-black water below bursts with the staccato of rain, layered with trills of exploding gunpowder, a rhythm of racing hearts. The song's refrain pierces the night sky.

What a beautiful anthem for a captive audience. Let's call them refugees, or are they fugitives? Heroes or traitors? Predator or prey? Depends on who is telling the story. Either way, into death they went, to seek life.

We're fucked, Lan thought.

The Vietcong police weren't supposed to be out. Most guards stayed on the shore during a raging storm. That was why tonight was chosen. This was supposed to be their ticket out of here. They had spent years preparing for this moment of escape. Now they were definitely going to die. The wind gusts whipped rain onto their already soaked bodies. Each passenger had swum a quarter mile out to the tiny fishing boat. But their thirteen-foot boat couldn't even make it out of the harbor. It had been only one hour. A taste of freedom. An amuse-bouche of hope followed by the main course of despair.

"Stop and surrender now, or we will kill all on board!" the guards shouted over a rusty, crackling megaphone. They needn't have announced themselves. Their guns already did the job.

In the night, through the fog, the siren grew louder and louder. A song of damnation.

Lan, my mother, knew what would happen next.

. . .

Sadness looks up from the pages. 15 and 5 are passed out from exhaustion by the fireplace. She closes the book.

"We should let them rest and continue this story tomorrow. You'll need the daylight for Acceptance's realm anyway."

I feel slumber's embrace, my eyelids heavy and my body sore from the storm. I nod in agreement. I sit in silence with Sadness. The fireplace crackles. I think about my mother.

14.

THE DECISION
TO LEAVE

The first time I walked into the rape crisis center, there weren't enough seats in the waiting room.

It was my first clue that my story wasn't mine alone. It was the story of more than a hundred thousand survivors in Massachusetts. Millions more across the country. And tens of millions around the globe. The full scale was incalculable, in the truest sense of the word. A countless toll of women, mostly suffering in silence, trapped somewhere in this cycle alongside me.

Were they fighting to save their rape kits, too? Did they even know that they had to? How many had given up hope? How many had stood and fought, only to be knocked down, over and over again? In spite of everything that had happened to me, I believe that people are fundamentally good. Most of them want to help—they just don't know how. But when you present them with hope, you find that hope is contagious. People rally to it. They fuel it. And hope spreads like fire.

Over the next several weeks, the response to my message is overwhelming.

I hear from friends, former co-workers, professors. Alice, a law student, will help draft the bill with me and Diane. David, a friend from college with a new job on Wall Street, will help calculate the economic impact of the bill. Ben will build a website. William, my former boss, connects me with two other bosses at the immigration nonprofit, Lisa and Scott, former senior staffers in Congress and the White House who encourage me to draft a federal bill alongside my Massachusetts bill. All of a sudden, my last desperate hope is paying off.

Most of all, I start to hear from survivors—both people from my life and strangers who forwarded the email or heard about it from a friend and decided to reach out. Women start sending me their stories from across the nation. Abby had her rape kit destroyed. Lindsey was thrown in jail to compel her testimony. Sarah was forced to pay for her rape kit. Mary's daughter was raped and murdered; her killer had first raped two other women whose rape kits were never tested; if they *had* been, one wonders if the police might have caught him in time. This was bigger than me, and bigger than just Massachusetts.

Diane, her students, and I talk with the women, read their stories, and ensure that these survivors find their voices, frustrations, and hopes reflected in the language of the bills we draft. This isn't a hypothetical exercise. Each right that we author corresponds to at least one real person who reached out to us, someone whose life was changed because a particular right was denied. Some rights are specific to the stories of one or two women. Some address indignities common to hundreds or more. My story began with the need to protect a rape kit from being destroyed—but we go well beyond that. We are composing a sexual assault survivor's Bill of Rights: a comprehensive declaration to fundamentally reinvent the way the system works—the right to not have our rape kits destroyed before the statute of limitations, the right to have access to our own patient medical records, the right to our own police report, the right to not have to pay for lifesaving medical services or our own evidence collection. Our goal is to ensure that no one has to go through what I went through ever again.

There are two bills, at first: a Massachusetts bill for the citizens of that state and a federal bill to extend those same rights to the twenty-five million rape survivors nationwide. The federal bill feels like a pipe dream, but we press on anyway. We owe it to these women who have endured so much and to those who, tragically, will join them someday.

*   *   *

Of course, just because we are working to break the cycle doesn't mean that the cycle has released me from its grip. I am still juggling, still trying to live, still trying to escape. I still have to secure a stable job to protect me from ever having to return to California—three thousand miles away, but still not far enough to let me feel safe from my parents. I do not have the luxury of waiting around to see if the CIA will pan out; I need a menu of options, a security net in case things fall through. If the East Coast doesn't offer me enough distance from the world I am escaping, perhaps outer space will do. I still harbor dreams of becoming an astronaut, so I apply to the White House in hopes of landing a political appointment at NASA. Those jobs, to say the least, are hard to come by, but I am willing to do anything to chase my dream. To get by in the meantime, I find a full-time job as a policy associate for a nonprofit organization. I balance this job with interviews at the White House, NASA, and the CIA, alongside the perpetual loop of trying to preserve my rape kit back in Boston, all while drafting a bill to change the laws of both Massachusetts and the nation. I pass out at my desk more nights than I make it into bed.

April 1, 2015

13 DAYS LEFT UNTIL KIT DESTRUCTION

It's 6:00 a.m. now. A newly purchased alarm clock sits on top of my white IKEA desk—a backup plan to my phone's alarm, a fail-safe to get me to the polygraph component of my CIA onboarding process. I'm getting close to the final phase now; the polygraph comes only after a candidate has been provisionally accepted. Both alarms should have woken me two hours ago. Neither one has done its job.

In my REM-stage nightmare, I am trapped in a room on fire. I hear my real-life alarms, manifesting in my dream as fire alarms that won't stop blaring. I'm trying desperately to turn them off. Then it clicks. The sound isn't coming from my dream.

I jolt straight up in the real world—a world no less on fire. *Shit! Shit. Shit. Shit. Oh my god. Oh my god. I am late to my polygraph. Fuck fuck fuck.*

I sprint out of the elevator into a taxi. It's forty-five minutes from my home to the CIA. I'm berating myself in the car ride.

I'd spent the night before the polygraph once again frantically firing off emails to the Cambridge police and the Massachusetts forensic lab, trying to confirm, for the third time through this cycle, whether my kit was going to be salvaged or destroyed.

I am exhausted. Long gone are the friends, hobbies, and activities I once enjoyed. I cannot talk to anyone about the CIA job—and I avoid talking to people as a rule, so as to avoid talking about my rape. I am spreading myself too thin and juggling far too much. Something was bound to drop; I didn't know it would come in the form of sleeping through my alarms.

No time to feel sorry for myself. I have to prepare.

Once a staple of spy thrillers, the polygraph exam is now known to be of dubious accuracy—so much so that evidence obtained in a polygraph exam typically isn't even admissible in a trial. Regardless of whether or not it detects lies, however, the test is still intimidating; if you're nervous, it's going to show. In fact, many professionals suspect that the real reason the CIA still uses the polygraph is simply to scare people.

My four-inch heels clack against the asphalt as I speed-walk into the undisclosed location of my CIA test site. These heels were pretty to look at, but they were absolutely the worst choice I could have made this morning. I hadn't really thought about the shoes—they just happened to be there by the door as I scrambled to make it out of my apartment. But now, I am full of regrets. Brimming over with anxiety just before a polygraph. Running late for the most terrifying interview in the world. And to top it all off, I'm strapped into uncomfortable shoes.

I barely have time to consider the questions that are truly gnawing at me. The biggest ones: *What if they ask about the rape? What if they ask about my newfound activism?* I had reported the rape on the many pages of security information they make all the accepted candidates fill out—our past travel history, all our foreign friends, any family members who are foreign nationals, any hospitalizations that I've had, which includes the rape kit procedure. I am afraid they will see the rape as a vulnerability. Before I can dwell further, I make it to the dark, cramped, windowless room—a claustrophobic shoebox of four asylum-white walls, lit by the alien glow of the polygraph device.

Wires spill out from its place on a desk in the corner where my interviewer sits behind a monitor. I take my seat perpendicular to him, staring straight ahead at the blankness of the wall. In the upper corner of the right wall a camera is tilted down. The interviewer is not the only one observing me.

During a typical exam, the interviewer tries to establish

a baseline for your behavior, a normal reading of your stress levels they can measure against. Only then do the wires get attached: electrodes on your fingers to measure your skin's electrical conductance, a blood pressure cuff, and two pneumographs across your torso to monitor your breath rate. They'll run another baseline test—*What's your name? Who's the president?*—and finally, the test begins.

Every survivor learns the art of "I'm fine"—the magic trick of getting through the day with a passable poker face, of keeping it together on the outside while a hurricane rages inside us.

Today, I am a Category Five.

I am consumed by fear—just the sort of vulnerability the CIA is looking for. Something that foreign spies can exploit or use as blackmail. I wanted to save my rape kit. My rape was a liability.

My anxiety is boiling as I answer the first round of questions, my body bracing for the moment when my rape will first be raised. My feet shift restlessly across the floor—a terrible indicator, I acknowledge to myself, even as I can't bring myself to stop. I find a faint gray smudge on the wall and draw my focus there to keep my eyes from dilating, hoping that the camera won't clock it as an effort to fight the polygraph. I'm overthinking things.

I reported the rape on my paperwork. I knew they were going to ask about it. When the question comes about my rape, there is no doubt what is happening to my heart. I feel it all: my breath speeding up, my heartbeat pounding, sweat pooling out, white-hot rage filling me up. I can practically hear the spasm of the polygraph needle, screaming to my prospective employer that this candidate is not doing okay. CIA officers must stay calm. I was anything but calm.

My taxi ride home feels even worse than the ride to the interview. I know why they asked about my rape, but it's hard not to feel like I'm being blamed for my own attack. They did not say it outright that I would be demerited for the assault. But it feels like they did. My exhaustion is mixed with anger. Anger at the CIA for asking the question. Anger at the criminal justice system for destroying rape kits. Anger at society for victim blaming survivors. Why should I be demerited for the violence that happened to me? In how many ways can survivors be judged, branded, and stigmatized for the rest of our lives? I am so much more than my rape. But to the institutions I'm counting on, it's a vulnerability. A weakness. A source of exploitation and compromise. A reason to turn me away.

I arrive back to my apartment and kick off my heels, stumbling to the bed to give my feet a chance to recover. Across the room, my teal folder—my Pandora's box—still sits on my desk. Next to it, an Excel spreadsheet laying out the legislative landscape for survivors in every state across the country, a jumble of rights, roadblocks, and precedents to aid my drafting of the bill. I pass out.

TIME REMAINING UNTIL EVIDENCE DESTRUCTION: 4 DAYS

It's April 10, 2015. I have four days left until my kit is destroyed. 5,760 minutes left. Time loop.

Six months later, I am right back where I was. Even if I am drafting a new law, even if the campaign is gaining momentum, even as we are collectively imagining this new world we're fighting for, I am still stuck in the current reality. In that current reality, rape kits are still destroyed after six months. Again, the game board shifts. I'm on those shifting stairs at Hogwarts. The first time I extended my kit, the rape crisis center contacted the state lab but refused to give me hard evidence unless I flew there in person to get it. The second time I extended my kit, I had to track down Gloria, a staff member at the state forensic lab who never addressed me as a human, via an out-of-office responder. I've now called Gloria again, who refuses to talk to me. Apparently there is a new rule that the staff cannot talk to victims and instead can talk only to lawyers, so I email Diane.

April 10, 2015

Hi Diane,

It's 6 months and I have to extend my kit again. I called the lab and they said that despite the extension it was removed to Cambridge Police. They said they knew this was wrong but didn't know why. I really don't like talking to the police. Last time they told me erroneous information too. The lab said they won't talk to me but only to attorneys. I'm going through re-traumatization right now so my friend who was listening in the phone call took notes. What should I do? I'm in Boston today until Tuesday. Could I meet and talk to you?

I don't know what to do. This is clearly a violation of their own abysmal protocol. She even admitted that this shouldn't have happened because there was an extension but when I asked for an email confirmation of the information she said she had to check with her authorities to see if she could email me or not. They are only worried about protecting themselves. I don't know what the status of my kit is and I don't know who to contact or who to believe because both CPD and HUPD have lied to me before.

Thank you,
Amanda

That familiar feeling comes rushing in—I am spiraling. I feel like I'm back in that polygraph chair, but this time I'm at home. I am fucking exhausted. Why can't she just email me? This is so stupid.

With every action, there is an equal and opposite reaction. When you're vulnerable and sharing your experience, it comes with both the good and the bad. My bad came in a familiar shape: my parents, who managed to find out about my rape despite my choice not to tell them. A mistake by the hospital stripped me of that choice. Somehow, for my follow-up visit about the rape kit, the hospital had called my parents' home phone number instead of my cell phone. When my parents called me, the first person who spoke was my dad. I had not talked to either of them in a long time, especially since he was still not allowed on campus. He opened by asking, "Were you drinking? What were you wearing? How did you let this happen to you?" His words seared scars in me that have never quite healed, unlike the physical scars he's left me. They thought that their Harvard-graduated daughter was throwing away her chances of any future career by even acknowledging a topic this taboo.

It wasn't only my parents. Those who genuinely cared for me also questioned putting my dreams on pause. Ellen, my astronaut mentor, encouraged me to seriously understand how difficult it would be to delay my astronaut journey dreams and come back at another time. What about my career? What about going to space? *What about my dreams?* I think. *Are survivors allowed to have dreams?*

I am crashing and burning juggling my nine-to-five job at the immigration nonprofit, writing two laws, saving my kit, and going through the onboarding process at the CIA. I have been struggling ever since my rape to not have to choose between justice and my career. But I now know in my heart that I cannot do both. I don't have the money, time, or energy. But before I make the choice, there's one person I need to talk to.

•   •   •

Leland Melvin was drafted by the Detroit Lions in the 1986 NFL Draft before he became a NASA astronaut. He is the only person to catch a football both in the NFL and in space. He is the perfect picture of what all little boys' dreams are. In fact, his official astronaut picture is one of the most famous— Leland snuck in his two dogs to be in the photo with him.

I first met Leland while interning at NASA HQ, where he was the head of education. Leland's story is one of second chances. At first, he was a talented athlete. When he got injured and had to stop playing, he became an astronaut. But everything almost ended before his next chance. Leland was training to perform a space walk at NASA's Neutral Buoyancy Laboratory, a five-million-gallon pool that simulates space's microgravity, when he realized something had gone wrong. Very wrong.

In his spacesuit, thirty-two feet underwater, he could not hear his instructor. As the team pulled him out of the water, Leland realized he was deaf. His suit was missing a Valsalva, a device that helps astronauts equalize air pressure. After an emergency surgery, Leland's hearing partially returned, but he was medically disqualified from his dream of spaceflight.

Leland turned to educating children about space. On February 1, 2003, Leland was on his way to work with teachers and students when Space Shuttle *Columbia* disintegrated coming back to Earth. To honor the legacy of his friends, he flew around the country to speak at different memorial services about their sacrifice for humanity. Unbeknownst to him, Rich Williams, NASA's chief flight surgeon, was observing Leland at every plane takeoff and landing. Rich signed a waiver for Leland to fly in space; Leland has since flown twice in Space Shuttle *Atlantis* as a mission specialist on missions STS-122 (2008) and STS-129 (2009).

I go to meet Leland at NASA HQ in DC. NASA HQ is unlike what any Hollywood film would have you believe. Like all government agencies, NASA is in DC because that's where all the decisions are made. The building is a regular government building, nondescript except for the iconic round blue logo, affectionately called "the meatball" by the space community. In the lobby, a gold Nobel Physics Prize is displayed under a spotlight and suspended over a rotating platform. Dr. John C. Mather and Dr. George F. Smoot won it for discovering the Big Bang through cosmic radiology research; I was lucky enough to meet Dr. Mather when I was an intern. In another corner of the lobby is a replica of Neil Armstrong's Apollo 11 suit. Down the corridors, colorful posters illustrate the various science and crewed missions the different departments are working on. Every mission has the coolest accompanying paraphernalia: a mission patch, models of a rocket or satellite. All of it instantly brings me joy, a feeling I haven't felt in so long. NASA is my happy place.

Past security, I turn right into the elevators and head to the top floor, where Leland's office is. The most beautiful kaleidoscopic pictures of our universe adorn the walls. The Hubble Space Telescope's breathtaking photos remind me of the orbital perspective, also known as the "overview effect," a term that's been documented in psychiatric literature as what astronauts who go to space experience. They have described it as being fully in awe of Earth—both terrified by its amazingness but also humbled by humanity's togetherness. It's essentially an existential crisis. They describe it as an overwhelming need to protect Earth, an understanding that we are all in this spaceship together. In space they can't see borders, but they can see how fragile our blue marble is. Astronauts leave Earth as technical people and return as activists.

Leland's voice rings through the air. "Amanda! Welcome back!"

I turn away from the Hubble photos and see Leland's smile; it tends to warm the souls of everyone around him. His positive energy is infectious. For a little bit, I feel like I can take a break from the dreariness of my nightmare. At NASA, with Leland, everything is possible.

"How are you? How's your pathway to astronaut candidacy?"

Last time I updated Leland, I was trying to get an appointment at NASA and then go back to school to continue my astrophysics studies to bolster my chances of becoming an astronaut. I brace myself to tell him what's happened, especially in light of what other people at NASA have told me about my activism.

Leland pauses and takes a deep breath after I tell him everything: the rape, the countdown to the kit destruction, the choice between a career and activism, the responsibility I feel I have to other survivors.

"I know how you feel, Amanda," he says. "I know because I'm also a survivor."

What? The. Leland. Melvin. Did I hear that correctly? The man who has it all. He's a survivor, too?

"It happened when I was a child."

Another pause. He starts again.

"Have you heard about Katherine Johnson?"

I shake my head.

"Katherine is my mentor. Katherine was a civil rights hero and human 'calculator' who helped the Apollo missions reach the moon. This was during the sixties. Space and civil rights have always gone hand in hand," he says with a smile.

"Space is going to be there. It's going to be there long after you're gone. So go fight for your civil rights, for our civil rights. And when you're ready, I'll be here to welcome you back to space."

•   •   •

Everyone has a hero. My hero is Leland Melvin. After our conversation I make my decision and step away from everything. I quit the CIA path. I postpone my astronaut dreams. Space will wait. I have to break away from my past in order to move forward. And there's only one way forward: taking on the US government and rewriting the law. I'm going all in.

15.

Let Go

Sunlight cascades in between the velvet curtains framing the windows of Sadness's lighthouse. I'm still on the chair next to the fireplace, ashes from last night's roaring fire smoldering. The smell of pancakes wakes my stomach. I turn my head to the sound of clanging utensils. It's 5, already up, scooping spoonfuls of cereal milk from a bowl of Cinnamon Toast Crunch. Sadness stands above the stove, nursing a brewed coffee.

15 is already fully clothed and standing by the door, tapping her foot impatiently.

"About time you woke up," she says. "We have to go back to find 22."

I swallow the spit in my dry mouth. My gaze turns back to 5 finishing breakfast, lifting the bowl to her face to drink every last drop of the milk. She nearly drops the bowl back onto the table, as if her arms can't bear the weight of it. I take a closer look at 5's face—it has started to turn purple.

"She's growing weaker. We have to finish the journey and take her to Acceptance before we lose 5, too."

"I'm not leaving 22 behind—"

"That's not what I'm suggesting," I interrupt 15. I see how heated she is still, kicking herself for not waking up early enough to find 22 even faster.

"Let's agree to split up," I say. "15, you go back to Bargaining to help search for 22, and I will carry 5 to Acceptance."

"I don't want to leave here!" 5 says. She swings her feet, which are dangling off the bench.

Sadness pours more coffee. She comes over to me. "Lost souls often stay in Sadness, but you have a mission. Save 5. I'll take you across the bridge to Acceptance's realm, and, 15, I will be here to help you cross the bridge when you come back as well."

With that, 15 opens the lighthouse door.

"Good luck, 15," I tell her as she steps out.

She pauses and turns back. "You, too." The door closes behind her.

I hoist 5 onto my hip. She rests her head on my shoulder. "We're ready. Thank you for leading us, Sadness."

In the bright daylight, I see what I couldn't in the storm. Sadness's lighthouse sits on cascading gray shale cliffs, contrasting against the blueness of the sky and the pastel stripes of the lighthouse. On the horizon, I see the red sail of the junk boat we were on and 15 making good headway back to

Bargaining's market. When I turn inland to the opposite direction, I see that the barren shale extends for a quarter mile. At the end of the realm is a long, rickety rope bridge. On the other side of the bridge, giant sand dunes loom. Below, the cliff drops into an abyss. We head toward the bridge.

"We'll make it. I promise we'll make it, 5," I whisper to her as I take my first steps on the bridge. The wooden planks protest under my feet. Thick, braided natural-fiber ropes hold up the suspension bridge; two load-bearing cables anchor it on both ends of the cliff.

Sadness must have sensed my anxiety. "Do you know how your mother's story ends?"

"Yes. It's a story she told us many times."

"We didn't get to finish it. Let me hold 5 for you. Read it for me as we walk." She pulls out my mother's book and hands it to me. I touch the pages, one hand holding the rope and the other finding the marked place, and begin reading as we walk through the grayness above the abyss.

* * *

In the storm of the harbor, Lan braced for the impact of the guards' boat. Through the night, their megaphone blared: "Prepare to be boarded!"

Lan gripped the hand of Sister 11. "We didn't even make it out of the harbor," Bach cried.

Brother 3 hushed them. "They have guns. Let's stay calm and take this step by step. We'll wait as they've asked."

Time passed by, and though the guards' boats were nearby, they had yet to board.

"What's going on? Are they preparing to kill us instead of taking us in?" Lan asked. In the distance, Lan made out the shape of a large ship—more refugees trying to escape.

"Stay where you are!" the guards yelled. "We will come back for you!"

"They are chasing the other ship! That boat is bigger. Maybe wealthier refugees who brought gold with them?" Lan exclaims.

Lan turned to Brother 3, the captain of their boat. "3, it's do-or-die. We must try to escape. We will likely be killed anyway when they bring us in. Better to fight for our chance to live."

In a split-second decision, Brother 3 turned on the engine. The boat raced forward into the night.

• • •

The last meal Lan ate in her homeland was forbidden. Refugees were not allowed to bring anything onto the boat. No food, no jewelry, no extra clothes. You had to look like you weren't trying to escape. If you carried too much, the Vietcong would know that you were trying to flee. But Lan was so hungry and so nervous. And that nem chua, sour garlic pork, looked so good.

Saigon had fallen. With its fall brought an exodus of refugees, escaping by air, land, or sea. Months earlier, the family had gathered around the dining table. A difficult decision lay ahead. Four members would be chosen to make the treacherous journey to escape. Chances of death were high. One could be caught by the Vietcong. Or pirates. Or swallowed by the sea.

Lan volunteered to go on the boat. She was the tenth out of twelve siblings. She loved her mom, and her mom was dying. The best chance of saving her was to escape. If Lan survived the trip, maybe she could sponsor her mother out of Vietnam to another country, where hopefully she would get better medical care. The final four were decided: Bach, Khoa, Khai, and Lan.

On the planned day of departure, Lan looked at her sister Bach, nicknamed Y Ut, or littlest sister.

"I'm so hungry," Bach said.

"We can't bring anything," Lan whispered. "We can't risk it."

"Just one last meal. People eat. People who are not trying to escape eat. We can eat."

So they bought some sour pork and sat by the dock, waiting for the night to settle in and the moonlight to guide them to their ark. Sisters going into death to seek life, eating a forbidden meal.

Vietnamese legend says the moon is a woman in love. Centuries ago, the world was burning because there were too many stars surrounding it. Hậu, a talented warrior, saved the world by vanquishing the stars. For his heroic task, Hậu was given the elixir of immortality. But Hậu wanted to share this elixir with his wife, Hằng Nga, so he hid the elixir in their home. One day, one of Hậu's disciples broke in to steal the elixir. He threatened to kill Hằng. Hằng drank the elixir to keep it out of the hands of the evil student. The magic immediately pulled Hằng into the sky and toward heaven. But her love for Hậu was so powerful that the goddesses let her stop at the moon so that she could still be able to see Hậu. There she lives with her rabbit, forever suspended in between the earth and heaven. Thus, in Vietnam, the moon represents love.

The night before Lan's journey she'd hugged her mother tight. "Look up at the moon, my daughter. No matter where we are on this planet, it will be the same moon," Lan's mother told her before Lan set sail to find a brave new world.

After Khai sped out of the harbor, the group evaded death's grip to find themselves in another catastrophe. The monsoon storm had created tidal waves. Their tiny fishing boat was sinking. A bigger boat came to rescue them. But because it was so big they couldn't drag the small, sinking fishing boat, or else it would smash into theirs. So the bigger boat threw over a single lifeline in the storm, and everyone had to climb. All four siblings climbed the rope and survived.

At the Malaysian refugee camp, Lan found an aid worker and asked to relay a message home that she, Bach, Khai, and Khoa had made it. It was nighttime when Bach ran back from the aid tent with a letter, the first message they received from Vietnam. Their mother had died—the whole reason Lan had volunteered to leave had been to save her. Lan made it to freedom, but she still couldn't save her mother. Bach and Lan took the letter and held each other on the beach as they cried.

Let Go

* * *

Deep breath. I close the pages of the book and look up. We've almost made it to the end of the bridge.

"Thank you for that story. I can't imagine how hard it was to read that, but I'm glad we're here at the end. Give me the book and you take 5."

I hand over the book as she places 5 on the bridge and holds her hand. She's able to walk, though stumbling a bit. As I reach the end of the bridge, a loud snap echoes throughout the cavern. Threads of the fiber have started to disintegrate— one by one they are snapping. I yank 5 off the bridge, and as I do, the bridge snaps completely, Sadness still holding on to the rope anchored to the edge of the cliff. Panicking, I push 5 toward safety and grab the remaining rope Sadness clings to.

"Let go," Sadness says.

"No! What! I cannot lose any more people today!"

Sadness insists. "Yes, you can. Let go of me. I've climbed out of this abyss many times before."

I refuse to believe her, but the rope continues to slip out of my hands. Alongside Sadness, a girl is clinging to the rope.

"Who is that?" I call out.

"This is 10," comes Sadness's reply.

"Is she—is it me? Another me, at 10?"

"Not this time," Sadness answers, and across the divide I recognize my mother as a child—my mother, sibling number ten—holding fast to the rope, as she had so long ago.

5 places her bruised, poisoned hand on me, and I let go.

16.

THE UBER RIDE

Today is the day. It's my first time talking to politicians to convince them to sponsor my bill, to convince them that survivors deserve human rights.

I've flown back to Boston for the meetings. I stomp in my heels with determined righteousness against the redbrick sidewalk outside the Massachusetts State House. Its gold-leaf gilded dome gleams in the sunlight against a bright blue sky. The gold that shines on the dome is the result of multiple re-gildings. The last time was in 1997; the twenty-three-karat gold cost taxpayers at least $1.5 million. The cost to store a rape kit indefinitely is less—next to nothing. It's funny how priorities are determined by our government.

The campaign has grown to a team of seventy volunteers across the country. We call ourselves Rise. I chose the name because it indicates momentum, to recognize that this campaign started from a dark place but is now moving somewhere brighter, up and away. The name also subtly references my love of space. A rising rocket ship. Our campaign has prepared extensively for this day. My arms wrap around fifteen folders. In the folders' pockets are multiple copies of the draft bill our Rise team has written with Diane, a legislative landscape of all the laws in the United States pertaining to survivors' rights, and an analysis of how the bill impacts the economy.

Alice, Shammas, MaryRose, and I are meeting at the entrance of the statehouse. We're the team going in to meet with the state senators. It feels like we're preparing to go meet with the sharks on *Shark Tank*, except the product is civil rights with implications for millions of people. Alice and Shammas are Harvard Law students from the Harvard Students for Reproductive Justice organization. MaryRose is a Harvard Kennedy student who used to work at the Massachusetts State House. Together we delineated our roles: MaryRose would use her credibility as someone who worked at the state house to indicate why this was a worthy political issue for the senators to support. Alice and Shammas would talk through the legal drafting of the bill. I would share the economic impact of the issue. MaryRose used her connections to convince several offices to meet with us, so we have a long day ahead.

My stomach rumbles with nerves as we walk across the tile floors to our first meeting. I spent yesterday thinking about what I should wear. *How do I present myself so that they'll take me seriously?* I know that it shouldn't matter, but my father's question about what I was wearing when I was raped echoes in my head. I'm used to debating how to balance my rage and despair with professionalism over email with the police, or with the state lab, so that I can save my kit. Now I'm coming face-to-face with actual politicians—people who were elected to serve the Commonwealth of Massachusetts, whose jobs are to listen to the problems of their constituents and make things better. I settled on a modest, deep navy blue dress that covers me to my neck and all the way down to my wrists. It seems like the team thought carefully about what to wear, too: MaryRose in a gray pantsuit, Alice in a black pantsuit, and Shammas in a navy pantsuit. We look like the best-dressed professionals in the state house or the most boring rock band.

I unfold my arms to hand out the briefing papers to the team. We've practiced our talking points over and over for the past few weeks, emphasizing core principles that are the same regardless of political party but that may hit deeper with different politicians. Republicans are more likely to resonate with the concept of justice, while Democrats are more likely to care about the experiences of victims. Above our agenda we have notes about each person we're meeting. This state senator cares about women's rights and voted for recent bills pertaining to the issue; this state representative has the forensic lab in their district and won their election by a small margin, most of whom were women. From their voting history, to their campaign promises, to their margin of victory— we've done our homework. Deep breath. My chest rises with optimism. We are determined. We are putting ourselves out there. This must be what hope feels like.

That hope quickly leaves, like a balloon popping. In our first meeting the staffer apologizes on behalf of the senator who promised to be there but couldn't show up due to a last-minute work conflict. Still, MaryRose begins with the pleasantries, while Alice and Shammas follow up about the bill. I present the statistics: Massachusetts has over one hundred thousand rape survivors. The government currently destroys rape kits at six months even if the statute of limitations is fifteen years. Other states have laws that prevent this from happening; there's legal precedence to keep the evidence instead of destroying it. Equality under the law should exist for survivors. Two survivors in two different states shouldn't have two completely different sets of rights.

One staffer seems preoccupied with checking their email. Another stifles a yawn. These legislative aides could not be more uninterested. With their body language and tone, they act as if they are Olympian gods giving us the grace of their time. We hand over the briefing folders.

"I'll make sure the senator sees this," one aide says with a half smile as he pushes out the office door, avoiding eye contact and looking at his watch.

The next few meetings follow the same pattern. It's midday, our fifth or so meeting. Something in my chest gnaws at me. Should I? Should I reveal that this isn't some Harvard theoretical experiment? That these rights reflect real people with real lives, real rape kits on the line? My stomach drops, the same feeling I get when a plane free-falls for a couple of seconds in turbulence.

Like an athlete zoning out the noise of the crowd before

they enter the arena, I still my adrenaline. As calmly as I can say it, I utter the words "I am a rape survivor."

Immediately the staffers' heads shoot up from their Black-Berries. My team turns toward me. There's silence in the room. Sitting to my right, MaryRose brings her hand up to mine and squeezes it.

"I am a rape survivor, and these numbers represent me. The worst thing that happened to me wasn't being raped. It was being betrayed by the Massachusetts criminal justice system. I went to the police. I went to the hospital. But I will still lose my evidence because this system has been designed to throw it away. My rape kit will be destroyed if this law doesn't pass. Thousands of survivors' justice will be destroyed if this bill doesn't become law. Will you help us?"

I hate this feeling, hate that I have to put myself out there, beg for my rights and share my trauma in order to get people to even pay attention. I know that as soon as I say the "R word," that's all I'll be seen as. The word is so weighted in taboo it erases the rest of my identity. I'm no longer any of my accomplishments, any of my work experience as a campaign organizer or a legislative analyst. I'm only a victim. But maybe that's what this process demands, I think; maybe I have to sacrifice myself in order to get anywhere. There's no turning back now.

"Of course," the aide says, shifting his shoulders forward. "Actually, the senator is coming in. Let me see if he can stop by and hear from you directly."

All of a sudden, this politician has time to meet. The aide leaves the conference room and returns with the senator. "Can you repeat what happened to you, Amanda?" the aide asks me. I do, my heart pounding, gripping MaryRose's hands even tighter. Alice and Shammas then share their legal talking points.

The senator stares at me. In the most saccharine, pedantic voice, almost as if he were talking to a child, he says, "Wow. That was so brave of you to share. I'm sympathetic to your cause, but my constituents don't know me for this issue. Thank you, though, so much, for sharing your story with me." His lips are pursed and his eyebrows are furrowed. He could have easily said, "Aww, poor baby," with the same face. I don't know how to react. My insides are jumbled. The plane is in free fall.

"Let's get a picture with you and the senator," the aide chimes in with a phone camera already up.

Flash.

I don't even have time to say yes or no. Will this picture be posted today somewhere? Are they going to label me as a survivor publicly? While I'm wondering, the senator has already stood up and walked out.

"He heard your voice today," the aide declares triumphantly. MaryRose, Alice, Shammas, and I nod in acquiescence.

The next meetings are the same. One state representative even says to us bluntly, "This isn't going to help me get reelected." I'm stunned at their lack of empathy. At least they're honest, I guess? At the end of our multiple hours of stomping through the state house, I'm left exhausted. I hug each member of the team goodbye on my way to the airport back to DC. The plane ride takes less than two hours.

Back in my studio apartment the weight from the day lifts, but I feel gutted. Like I had to spill the entrails out of my body, showcase how damaged they are, and then neatly package them all back inside, serving my terror on a platter, in a consumable way in order for the people who have been elected to care. Look at this damaged organ. It's bad, isn't it? Look at how rape kits are destroyed. It's bad, isn't it? It feels like I'm only there to perform my pain for voyeurs. My trauma is on the menu to be consumed. The main course is the violence on the meat of Amanda, garnished with a broken criminal justice system. The literal legal bill is a side thought at the end.

Could it be that I will only be able to win my human rights if I suffer for their enjoyment? Is it true that victims only matter if we're politically beneficial?

"God, I just need one person to tell me that they love me," I beg and cry on my bed, holding my space shuttle plushie. I am alone, devoid of parents to call. An exoplanet poster hanging above my mattress watches over me as I pass out.

But I'm quickly learning that being an activist requires being a pathological optimist. The next morning, I get up, pick up the same fifteen folders, practice the same talking points, wear the same modest navy dress, and head to another legislative body, this time to the US Senate. Another time loop, but this time it's of my own creation.

The Rise team had drafted both a Massachusetts bill and a US federal bill because I live in DC and can take meetings on the Hill. Less than 1 percent of bills became law in the previous session of Congress. The federal bill is a crapshoot because statistically nearly all bills that are introduced die, but so is any law, including the Massachusetts one. This campaign is an experiment in hope, so we shoot our shot at it all.

The truth is that I am in denial. My rage drives me, and there is no other way out. I am not going to accept injustice, so the only option left is to pass this law. I had quit everything else to focus on this, including the most precious thing to me: my dream of going to space. How ironic, I thought, that I would have to give up my identity to work at the CIA. Instead, I'm giving up my identity to serve my country in a different way—by becoming an activist.

This is the only thing on my horizon now. I eat, sleep, and dream of the bill day and night. From eyes open to eyes closed. My former bosses at the immigration nonprofit—William, Lisa, and Scott—had all encouraged me to talk to the US senators about the federal bill, too. Luckily their friendship stretches across party lines. All of them had extensive backgrounds as senior staffers on the Hill in both Republican and Democrat offices before they led the nonprofit. They saw me suffer through the multiple times I had to fight for my rape kit extensions. When I'd asked them for help, they immediately said yes. Their encouragement gives me the delusional belief that I could meet with actual US representatives.

My first time begging politicians to care about rape survivors depleted my energy. The conversations took so much out of me. It felt like I was still gathering my entrails and placing them back in my body, preparing for another regutting. I tap my phone screen, putting my Uber destination as the "US

Capitol." I stand in the circular driveway of my Chinatown apartment complex waiting for the car in the same dress I wore yesterday. The recent addresses that pop up in the app show NASA HQ and the DCA airport. I've traded my NASA trips for trips to the US Capitol. And today, I am going in alone since most of the team is in Massachusetts.

A sedan pulls up, and I hop in. The driver is a big man. If he stood up he'd easily be over six feet. He doesn't say hello, which is fine. I don't have much energy to talk; my anxiety is starting to build again. It's a quick ride without traffic, about seven minutes from my apartment to the Capitol. I see him glance down at the map that routes us to my destination. We've stopped at a red light.

"Why are you going to the Capitol?" he asks in a gruff voice.

Should I tell him the truth? I should get used to it, right? Exposure through repetition. Maybe I can get my soul to a point where it is calloused over and talking will hurt less. I'm about to say it to a bunch of strangers on the Hill. I can practice talking about it here.

I blurt out the story of my rape. Immediately after, I can't believe I said everything I just said to a complete stranger I met seconds ago. He doesn't respond. We turn onto Constitution Ave, and the car stops at my destination. The driver turns around and looks me straight in the eyes. I see now he hasn't responded because he's clearly been holding back his emotions.

"My daughter is a rape survivor. And what you went

through, she also went through, too." Tears are welling out of his eyes. "Can I shake your hand? Thank you so much for fighting for her."

A stream of tears rushes down my face, too. This compassion and grace are what I asked God for after my first trip pitching the bill. We reach for each other's hands and shake firmly. His hands are leathery but soft. I wipe my tears and gather my briefing packets. As I touch the handle to open the door, he says, "Has anyone told you that they love you today? I love you."

I'll never forget that dad.

17.

The Reflection

The brightness of the white dunes blinds me. We walk, without direction, into the desert to find Acceptance. For as far as I can see, wavelike, white gypsum dune fields stretch to the horizon. There are no milestones. The sun is scorching, and 5 and I are both thirsty, dirty, scratched-up, and shaken from Sadness's fall. The food Anger has given us is long gone. The wind picks up and whips granules across my body. It feels like a sandstorm is about to emerge.

I pick 5 up, walk to the shadow of a dune for shelter, and fall into the sand. I am exhausted and sore, body and spirit. We sit in silence for some time.

"What do you think Acceptance is going to ask us when we find him?" I ask 5.

"Probably something about acceptance. 'What's the hardest thing you've had to accept?'" 5 postulates. We both laugh and say at the same time: "Dad." I look back up to the sky, too tired to turn my head.

"Tell me about Dad," 5 insists.

Sand shuffles in the wind at my feet. I hesitate to answer. Finally: "I thought maybe if I could change the world, I could change Dad, too."

I hear 5 stir and crane my neck to see what's going on. Out of her denim overalls, she retrieves a book.

"You took Dad's story from the lighthouse library?"

"Yeah. It was next to Mom's." She smiles wearily. "Read it to me."

Saigon, April 1975

Tu Nguyen, Dad, was a brilliant painter. He was sixteen years old, the youngest of six siblings, and lanky. He excelled in math and computer science and, unexpectedly, was an excellent artist.

Tu stared at his paintbrushes.

BOOM!

A siren shattered his fixation. Tu's auntie Thuy, who served as a representative in the Republic of Vietnam, was friends with President Nguyen Van Thieu. Auntie had known that Saigon was going to fall. She gave her brother, Tu's father, only a couple hours' notice.

"You need to leave now. There's no time to pack. The Americans have arranged a C-130 military aircraft escort for you to leave the country," she told him.

"TAKE NOTHING. GET IN THE CAR!" Tu's dad bellowed to him and his siblings.

"There will be brushes in America," Auntie Thuy insisted as Tu stared longingly at his supplies.

He squeezed in the car. Through the window, he took one last look at his home. Then the car sped through the streets of Saigon.

Tu found it understandable to leave his painting materials behind, but he also wondered if he could keep his real name and age. During the war, his mother had stripped him of his real name in order to protect his older brother from the draft. Why she made Tu do it, too, even though his young age made him safe from the draft, he didn't and still doesn't understand. Tu had always felt alienated from the rest of his family, mainly because of a rumor that he looked more like his uncle than his dad. This was a rumor his mother would mentally and physically punish him for, even though it wasn't his fault.

At the Tan Son Nhat International Airport, the Lockheed C-130 sat, loudly spinning its four turboprop engines across its 130-foot wingspan. The aft loading ramp waited for the family to board. Tu climbed up the ramp into the cargo bay, following the instructions of the American soldiers as they shouted. Red folding seats were attached to the wall. He flipped one down next to Thuy and strapped the harness and seat belts on. His fingers gripped the belt. Maybe the tighter he clutched it, the more he could squash the sound of his heart pounding, the trembling of his hands, the shortness of his breath.

There was no time to fear, to feel. No time to comprehend that loss sounded like a C-130 fleeing Saigon, a name that the city itself would lose. Loss of a name. Loss of a country. Loss of an identity. Loss of a childhood. Loss of innocence.

The C-130 flew from Saigon to Guam, where over a hundred thousand refugees were processed for resettlement under Operation New Life. From Guam, Tu's family was placed in Minnesota. In America, his mother still registered him with his fake age, ten years younger than he really was. Even as a gifted student in Vietnam, Tu was placed in lower grades in order to hide his age. To prove himself beyond his language barrier in his new country, Tu focused on math and engineering. Numbers and equations were some of the few things that transcended the borders he crossed. Engineering, especially aerospace engineering, was in turn easier to learn than English. Tu was a gifted engineer. He grew up around his father fixing televisions and radios in Vietnam. His academic excellence made him a favorite of professors, which led him to become a teaching assistant. He quit college after he was offered an engineering job and was able to chart his own path to the American dream. In America, Tu's love of painting took a back seat to survival, but his resentment grew.

Tu's love of painting eventually came back to him. Years later, after he became a software engineer, his artistic outlet took on a different form. His materials were still the same as they were in Vietnam. Brushes for painting, plaster for sculpting. But there were new tools, too. Instead of painting park scenes, he painted the house with holes from his fists, his anger coloring the walls. He sculpted his pain into the people around him. His daughter became his favorite painting, a canvas that could heal so that more and more paintings could be made. Ink from blood and bruises.

*　*　*

I pause the story.

"He started off as a hero," I tell 5, "but he still is a hero. He's a hero and a monster. It's common, you know, for people to love those who hurt them. It's not so straightforward. He was a lovable boy once, who was brave to escape. But his pain never did escape him and he put it on us instead."

I take 5's hand. "All fathers start off as heroes to their daughters. Our father is no different. In my dreams he is safe. Safe from his parents. Safe to be around. Safe to love. Safe to share my dreams with. Safe to share my heartbreaks with, without them being weaponized back at me in some way. In my dreams, he is finally my father. In reality, when I am awake, he is still Dad."

She nods. "I'm sorry I can't reach back in time to protect you from him."

As I finish speaking I catch something glistening in the distance. An oasis.

I pick up 5 and run to the body of water. I splash around, drinking voraciously from it. The cool liquid on my face feels like nirvana.

As the water ripples and calms, I notice 5's reflection. The poisoned veins have started to crawl up her small face. Something doesn't look right. I look closer at the water. A reflection is missing. I cannot see myself; only 5's reflection shines back. I touch the ripples in the water and wait for it to settle again. It still reflects back only 5.

"I was waiting until you'd notice." 5 smiles. "I am Acceptance."

18.

HONEY

Passing a law is like playing a game. In order to win any game, you need to know the rules. There's a board, there are players, there are basic rules. Then there are advanced rules. In Congress, there are even unspoken rules.

First, the game board. Congress is our game board. It's divided into two chambers: the House of Representatives and the Senate. Next, the game piece: the bill. A bill is a baby law, an idea that is drafted into legalese, which then is debated, shaped, amended, and voted on. The objective of the game is to move the bill forward through both chambers to become a law before time runs out. Bills take multiple tries through each legislative cycle to win. The average is five to seven cycles, or ten to fifteen years.

How is the piece moved through the game? Votes. There are four key votes to move a bill forward through Congress:

House committee vote, House floor vote, Senate committee vote, and Senate floor vote. The language of the bill in both chambers must match before it is sent to the president's desk for a signature.

Finally, the players. The players are the congressional members and senators who sponsor, draft, and vote on the bill. In this version of the game, all players are playing the game in service of a greater good—creating a more perfect union for the United States of America. Easy peasy.

Those are the basic rules of the game. You know how to pass a law, if the game existed in a perfect world.

Now for the advanced rules.

The advanced rules account for the real way the game is played. The game board is not only Congress—it's also the media. Congressional members and senators are not the only players. The roster has expanded to include activists, journalists, lobbyists, and celebrities. In the simple version of the game, everyone's objective is the same: pass the bill. In the advanced version of this game, people's objectives can vary. Some politicians may feign that it's their objective to pass a law, but in reality their objective may be to stay in power, get reelected, or become famous. Fewer than 1 percent of all bills introduced in Congress become laws because, well, the objective wasn't actually to pass it.

In any other industry, this abysmal failure rate would result in the firing and complete overhaul of the industry. But politicians—the most powerful people in the United States, the people who write the rules of how our lives are governed—have successfully convinced citizens that this performance is normal. It's more theater than legislation. That's why the playing field isn't just the legislative game board—it's also storytelling. It's the media, which includes social media. In an attention economy, the game pieces are the bill and the press.

This brings us to the unspoken rules of Congress.

Secret Rule One: Out of the 535 members, both representatives and senators, there are only four people in Congress who matter. They are called the agenda holders. Agenda holders are the gatekeepers of the process. Ninety-nine percent of bills die because the agenda holders don't put the bill on the agenda to be voted on. That's it. The four agenda makers are the Speaker of the House, the Senate Majority Leader, and the House and Senate chairs of the committee your bill is assigned to. Only these four can move the bill forward. All other representatives and senators just convince them. In a time before email and social media, sure, we would elect our representatives and they would then be able to talk to one of these four people. But in today's age, you can email or call the four decision-makers directly. Target the agenda holders.

Secret Rule Two: The lead sponsor of your bill should be a member of the majority party. Agenda holders are the leadership of the majority party. Compromise is the "C word" in DC. People are allergic to it. Political polarization has grown to an all-time high, and there are few incentives to work across party lines. Bipartisanship is often akin to giving the other party a win, so there is little reason for a majority party member to advance a minority party member's bill. Therefore the lead sponsor of your bill should be a member of the majority party.

Many politicians will send activists like myself on a fool's errand, telling them to rack up co-sponsors on their bill. While having a lot of co-sponsors may be a nice thing, it's not a necessary thing. If what you're fighting for is time-sensitive, if people's lives and justice are on the line, why waste time making the case that your bill is popular? Unless, of course, the objective isn't actually to pass the bill but rather to climb the political ladder or become famous. Most political campaigns virtue signal without substantive results. Most bills that are introduced are called "press bills," an excuse for politicians to stage elaborate press conferences, interviews, and media spreads to say that they care about an issue. They are sponsoring it! They'll stand next to victims and proclaim how they are fighting for the people! People should donate to their campaign so that they can fight for the cause more! But look a little closer. Is the politician a member of the majority or minority party? Because if they are a member of the minority party and they are the bill's lead sponsor, they've poisoned the well. Look at their track record. Have any of them lead-sponsored—not co-sponsored but lead-sponsored—a bill that successfully became a law? Most politicians who run for president of the United States have successfully passed zero or one law in their entire career.

It's easy to dupe people when they don't know the rules. There is a difference between feeling good and doing good. Congress is less about the latter and more about the former. Yelling feels good. Rage feels good. Compromise does not feel good. But true legislation demands compromise:

people with different views hashing ideas out, reasonably thinking through differences.

Now, these rules are secret for a reason—they aren't hard and fast. There are variances, and some might disagree. But knowing this background will increase your chances of winning. Many activists come to Congress thinking they are passing a law the normal way. But politicians are playing an entirely different game with an entirely different set of rules.

I believe that most politicians and activists start off as public servants, people who genuinely want to do good for their community. Along the way, the game chews them up and spits them out. They become reality TV stars for the world's most dangerous and important show, the 24/7 news cycle. How does someone navigate this system without getting lost? By having a clear north star. Few do.

I didn't have the luxury of a cathartic performance for some lawmaker's benefit. I had six months to save my rape kit. My justice was on the line, as well as that of twenty-five million rape survivors in the United States. Justice was my north star.

June 2015—US Senate

We have limited time to get the bill passed before the US legislative session ends. Since 2016 is a presidential election year, analysts project that the legislative session will stall as we inch toward November. Our team has been community organizing for a year now to mixed results. The Massachusetts bill has stalled, but amazingly, the US federal bill has gained ground. Usually, it's the other way around. State bills can pass more quickly than federal bills. But location matters, and since I am in DC, I have spent every waking moment meeting on Capitol Hill. Progress happens where you invest your time. We've secured bipartisan sponsors in the House of Representatives: Representatives Mimi Walters and Zoe Lofgren. Now we have to secure a Senate sponsor in order to actually have a fighting chance.

A couple months after I start Rise I meet Freya, a survivor who was also raped by Melanie's rapist. Freya soon becomes Rise's chief of staff and my right-hand woman. We spend many late nights researching legal precedence, training the team, and talking to survivors to build the federal campaign.

To build momentum for the federal bill, Freya and I reach out to experts in the grassroots-organizing world for advice. While many are sympathetic, they cannot support us due to their bandwidth. Nearly all warn us that federal legislation is impossible.

Some conversations are hard to forget. Upon hearing our survivors' stories and what we are fighting for, one nonprofit staffer tells us to "get the fuck off our turf." Freya and I are shocked. We politely but abruptly end the conversation, then sit in silence before debriefing. Did she *really* just say that to us? We assume that people working on similar issues will be more open to understanding our stories, but what we find is that many feel like legislation is a zero-sum landscape. That our fight for our human rights will somehow deter them from getting funding or their issues prioritized.

I couldn't allow myself to get discouraged. Despite what

others told us, my justice was on the line. There was no *try*. I had to fight for my kit. We pressed on.

Freya and I spend the weekend sending hundreds of emails to every single congressional office we can find. We receive rejection after rejection. But like everything in life, changing laws is about persistence. All it takes is one person to say yes. During my lunch breaks from work I go to the Hill and meet with anyone who will listen. From the intern in the hallway to a staffer who has only ten minutes. That's how we were able to secure sponsors in the House of Representatives. Now we have to secure one in the Senate. Our constant emailing finally pays off. Chad, a legislative aide from a Senate office, agrees to meet with us.

The Hart Senate Office Building is of a modernist architectural style. It stands out from the other neoclassical buildings that make up the Capitol. On the outside, white marble from Vermont shines nine stories high. Inside, Senate offices along the walls surround a lofty atrium. Visitors have to crane their necks to look at the skylight. The elevator doors are cast in bronze. The structure evokes a feeling of grandeur and hope.

Sounds echo upward as my heels tap against the rose-colored Tennessee marble floor of the atrium. The last time I was in these heels, I was running to my polygraph. Same shoes, different venues. Both the CIA's and the Senate's missions are about serving America's highest ideals. It feels scary to be doing that from outside rather than inside the system. But protesting is a valid way to love my country. This is my way of serving America.

We got lucky with our House sponsors. Both Representatives Lofgren and Walters are on the House Judiciary Committee. Our bill, the Sexual Assault Survivors' Bill of Rights, would be assigned to the Judiciary Committee here in the Senate, too. Chad's senator is not the ideal person to move it forward: they are not on the committee and not part of the majority party, but they are the first person in the Senate who has shown interest, and we will meet with anyone.

The bronze elevator doors open, and I walk into the waiting room of Chad's senator.

My arms wrap around a white binder. In the pockets are multiple copies of the federal draft bill, a legislative landscape of all the laws in the United States pertaining to survivors' rights, and an analysis of how the bill would positively impact the US economy. We've also added, with their consent, the stories of survivors from across the nation and how this bill will change or could have changed their fate. It is both the moral and strategic reasons for why survivors deserve rights.

Chad greets me with a warm smile. "Amanda! It's nice to meet you."

He isn't much older than me, early twenties with light brown hair. Chad's dressed in business-formal attire, sans the jacket. His white collared shirt is wrinkled but neatly tucked into his dress pants. We sit down in a small conference room. In the center a large conference table is surrounded by ten seats. He takes a seat at the end of the table and beckons to me to sit adjacent to him.

"It's just me today," Chad says, still smiling.

I slide him the packet of briefing materials my team has prepared for him. Without the team, I'm performing the full pitch. I'm Alice, Shammas, and MaryRose combined.

He fingers through the pages as I begin my spiel:

"Rape is the most expensive violent crime. Domestic violence pushes many women into poverty. The United States would add $4.3 trillion to the GDP if they invested more in women's equality. Investing in women is investing in everyone. Violence against women costs the United States a lot of money: $3.1 trillion over the course of a population lifetime for rape and $8.3 billion annually for domestic violence.

"It does not cost anything additional to leave rape kits where they are currently. Barriers to access justice, however, are a real economic burden. Rape is the costliest crime for victims. A National Institute of Justice study estimates that the annual costs to victims in the United States is $127 billion. These costs include both the direct medical and criminal justice costs resulting from the assault and other economic harms to the state. For example, one study estimates that fifty percent of sexual violence victims had to quit or were forced to leave their jobs in the year following their assaults.

"A 2017 study by the Centers for Disease Control (CDC) estimates that the lifetime economic burden of rape per victim is $122,461, which includes the cost of physical and mental health treatment, lost work productivity, and other factors. The White House Council on Women and Girls found in a 2014 study that the cost ranges from $87,000 to $240,776 per rape, which accounts for costs such as medical and victim services, loss of economic productivity, and law enforcement resources. Injustice is expensive. The Sexual Assault Survivors' Bill of Rights is an important step toward minimizing the economic impact of sexual assault on Americans."

"Wow . . . look at you," Chad says. "You've really done so much work here. Did you write this by yourself?"

Is that a genuine compliment laced with subtle condescension? I can't tell. What's more important is that he seems eager to support us. And we absolutely need a senator to introduce the bill.

Chad continues. "Made it easy for me. Usually, I listen to victims and then have to go back and do the analysis and then draft the bill. But you've got everything here. This is an easy win."

"Oh?" I blurt out, genuinely surprised. "That's so nice to hear. Everyone has said that it'll be difficult, that the rate of bills passing is only one percent . . ."

Chad seems so eager he doesn't hear me. He's lost in thought, circling the points I made on the paper. No one has been this eager before. I'm somewhat hopeful.

With excitement in his voice Chad proclaims, "The senator really cares about women. They're up for reelection, and this is going to be great, especially as they are on the campaign trail. I will push this upward. I bet they'd love to meet you and grab a photo. Let's set up a date."

I'm so thrilled that he's jumping at the opportunity. His positivity fills me with actual belief. Finally, after the hundreds of emails Freya and I have sent, we have a breakthrough.

"Have you shown this to anyone else?"

"You're the first!" I tell him.

"Good, good. I'm sure it's been hard. Not many staffers will get it. They only care about the hot-button issues. They won't understand you like I do. Let's keep this between you and me for now. I know the Senate, and you don't want to get this in the wrong hands. Don't reach out to anyone else. I'm happy to help guide you."

We get up from the conference table. I've left several folders behind so Chad can share them with his colleagues.

"I'm so grateful for your help," I say, beaming at him.

Chad smiles back, his eyes on the papers.

* * *

In the hallway of the Hart building, I speed-dial Freya to get her on the phone.

"Freya! I have *great* news."

"Me, too!"

"You do?"

"Scott and Lisa heard back from the chair of the Judiciary Committee. The decision-maker. They want to meet."

"Oh my god!" I screech, walking out of the Hart building. "But wait, I just had a great meeting with Chad. I think we have a chance of getting their support. But he said not to talk to any other offices."

Freya laughs. I can hear her gentle snark through the phone. "Well, this came in technically before you met him. Plus, he can't gag us. That makes no sense to not talk to anyone else. We've briefed the entire House of Representatives. It's *our* survivor stories and *our* rights. If his senator cares about this, they'll welcome the opportunity to talk to the other side and bring more support on board. Plus, the chair of Judiciary is a big deal. Chad's office isn't even on Judiciary. This is the best shot of us passing the bill."

Freya is right. This is a huge deal. Even our sponsors in the House weren't in majority leadership. To gain the support of the Senate Judiciary Chair would turn our campaign from a dream to surefire reality. It would mean twenty-five million rape survivors are closer to having rights.

. . .

The senior counsel who agrees to meet with us from the Senate Judiciary is Maria. Maria's senator is one of the most powerful politicians in America and one of the most senior in the US Senate. Senators are often too busy to run the day-to-day. It's the staffers who present the options. One could say she's the real decision-maker behind that power. By proxy, Maria is the most powerful person we have a scheduled meeting with. She could change everything. If we are able to surmount this challenge—even if not to get a sponsorship but to have the senator's blessing—we have an actual chance of winning.

The fact that Scott and Lisa put their reputations on the line so that I could have a chance to talk to Maria means the world to me. I also know how busy the senator and Maria are, so Freya and I prepare for our meeting with Maria like no other. I memorize the talking points so that I can make more eye contact instead of reading from the papers. It is a double-edged sword: The more we prepare, the more mythical and scarier Maria seems. In the back of my mind, I worry that Chad will find out and we'll lose his junior senator's support. Navigating political sensitivities and rivalries between politicians feels like an act of balancing delicate teacups stacked upon one another, all while playing hopscotch. But Freya and the other survivors keep my mind on the right path. No one owns rape survivors' issues, and we are not there to serve a random senator who only might help us.

Maria's office is in the Dirksen Senate Office Building, which could not look more different from Hart. Whereas Hart is an open atrium with light beaming through every window, Dirksen has low ceilings and is dark and imposing. The deep green marble and dark polished walnut wood absorb any outside light that peeks in through the heavy bronze doors. The buzzing fluorescent lighting does nothing to alleviate the heavy atmosphere. Outside, fifty-one bronze reliefs surround the building. They feature workers, all male figures, in five industries: shipping, farming, manufacturing, mining, and lumbering. It all gives off an air of classic prestige, but more in an intimidating secret lair kind of way, a lair for the country's most powerful people. The architecture screams: *There are important people walking here. Don't make eye contact. Get out of their way.*

Freya and I hope for the best but brace for a difficult meeting. Given the high stakes, we write talking points for every possible outcome, even rebuttals to things that seem ridiculous. What if she reacts callously to our stories? What if she brings up rapists' rights?

Scott joins me to meet Maria. As I pass through the bronze doors and metal detectors, Scott is standing next to the gilded elevators in a gray suit. There's a sign for all the office numbers, but he doesn't need to look at them. He knows where each office is by heart. Scott is tall and speaks with a deep South Carolina drawl. In another life, he could have become a radio announcer. His charismatic voice commands authority because, in truth, he actually has it. Scott's decades of service in the US Senate mean he knows everyone. I'm so lucky to have him and Lisa to help. While I was working for the advocacy nonprofit, Lisa and Scott had personally seen me in agony, begging the Massachusetts government to save my rape kit. When I decided to pursue changing the law, nearly everyone thought it was impossible except for them, because passing laws is simply what he and Lisa do.

This is the most important meeting of my life, but to Scott it's a regular Tuesday. I follow him as he navigates by memory to the Senate Judiciary Committee. The front desk attendants usher us into a conference room. The door handle turns. My heart jumps. Maria arrives.

I hear her through the door before I see her. She is busy, running from another meeting to make this one. In my mind she is a big, scary lawyer I have to get past, but in reality she looks like a caring person. Her strawberry blond shoulder-length hair, slightly disheveled, falls onto her cardigan. She smiles at me.

"Thank you for coming in to meet with me. Tell me your story."

This is the moment. I've memorized and prepared. I make eye contact. I share what happened and provide the talking points. Maria nods along and peppers my points with "mhmm"s to show she's actively listening. She jots down notes throughout my talk while referencing our brief in the folder.

When I finish, Scott, with his commanding voice, thanks her. "Maria, we know how busy the senator is, and we're grateful for your time."

"Oh, it's not an issue at all. I don't know if you know this, but before I came to the Senate I was the vice president of RAINN."

It dawns on me that although Freya and I researched everything there was to know about the senator, we didn't profile Maria herself. RAINN, the Rape, Abuse & Incest National Network, operates the nation's largest hotline for rape survivors. I didn't realize that she was already an expert on this specific issue.

"I care deeply about this issue, and I'll make sure the senator does, too. I read the materials you sent over."

She? Prepared? To meet with *us*? Am I dreaming? Is this for real? Her senator is the most important senator who could make a difference. Wow, she actually cares.

In the back of my head, Chad's meeting still weighs on me. I decide it's best to tell Maria, even if they are of different parties. "I met with another office, too. They seem to be supportive, and the staffer, Chad, is seeing if his senator will back it."

"Huh. That's interesting . . ." Maria pauses for a bit.

"Chad's senator isn't even on the Judiciary Committee. But it's okay, I'll figure out a way to work together."

* * *

I'm standing on a velvet carpet in a big fancy room, about to meet with Chad's senator. There is a photographer with a heavy-duty camera and big flashbulb around his neck. Chad also has his phone up. The senator comes out. We sit at a large polished wooden desk, and I begin sharing my story.

"Thank you so much for meeting with me today, Senator. It means so much to me. During my last semester of college, I was raped—"

Flash flash flash.

"And I went to the hospital, where my body was examined and prodded. Since the crime scene is my body. It took many hours—"

Flash flash flash.

"I found out that my rape kit, like many others, can be destroyed before the statute of limitations . . ."

Flash flash flash.

A nauseous feeling spreads in me, similar to the one I felt in Massachusetts. This meeting is more of a photoshoot than a chance for me to meaningfully talk about moving the bill forward. I feel like a prized pig being put on a pedestal for my pain to be observed—in awe, in horror, in delight. When the meeting ends and the senator leaves, I rush to pull Chad aside.

"That was great!" Chad beams at me. "There are some good photos there."

"Yes, thank you so much for arranging the meeting. But can we talk about the bill? I met with the Senate Judiciary Committee, with Maria, who is the legal counsel for *the chair*. She said they would sponsor it! You can work together across the aisle."

Chad stares at me. "No way you got a meeting."

"I know, right? To have the chair champion this would mean a real chance of the bill passing, of rape survivors getting civil rights, of my rape kit being saved."

Chad lowers his voice. "Amanda, I don't treat other activists the same way I treat you. Stop talking to other offices."

He follows me out of the carpeted office back down to the marble floors of the atrium. When I exit Hart, an involuntary chill runs down my spine.

April 2016

I know the rules. The staff knows the rules. The senators know the rules. The rules are: a member of the majority party, preferably an agenda holder like the chair of the committee your bill is assigned to, is your best chance of your bill passing.

That means Maria's senator, above all other senators, is the most powerful person who can ensure the bill is put onto the agenda in the Judiciary Committee and voted on. If he is the sponsor, it gives twenty-five million survivors a chance at justice. It gives me the chance to save my rape kit.

Waiting at this point is doubly agonizing: I'm attempting

to extend my kit and to count the time left before the legislative session ends and we have to start over. We wait to hear from Maria or Chad. The clock ticks closer and closer to the end. During my lunch breaks, I walk to Dirksen just to be around.

"I happen to be in the area. Any chance Maria is free?" I ask the front desk. "No worries if she's not!"

They always politely smile back. Maria isn't free, but they will make a note for her that I came.

One evening my phone buzzes. The caller ID reads "UN-KNOWN." It's either spam or the US Senate. My heart stutters; I pick up the phone. Maria is on the other line.

"Hey, Amanda, I'm sorry I missed you when you stopped by. I have bad news. Chad's senator has introduced the bill. I haven't been able to reach him."

"What?" I can barely get the word out. His senator, a member of the minority party, has poisoned the well by introducing the bill themselves, all but killing our chances. Chad's boss is not in the judiciary, nor are they in a leadership position, nor are they . . . they don't *care* if the bill passes. My stomach drops in free fall.

I rush to my laptop and google to see if the introduction has been posted anywhere. What is supposed to be a joyous moment turns into a swirling disaster: there I am in a press release at the wooden polished table on the fancy carpet, my mouth in the middle of speaking, in the middle of tearing my soul open. This is a press bill, nothing more.

"The chair isn't very happy about this," Maria says, sighing. "It's well outside of decorum. We're genuinely perplexed why this would happen, and quite honestly we would have welcomed a more thorough conversation about this before they decided to do it on their own."

"I'm so sorry . . . Maria. I didn't . . . I didn't know."

"Look, I'll try to talk with my boss. See what we can do. Perhaps there's a way we can put it as an amendment to another bill, make an exception so these civil rights won't die this session. I won't make a decision without making sure that you feel heard and survivors' voices are included."

I had kept my distance from Chad, ever since he threatened me in an attempt to cut me off from talking to other senators. But I know I have to call him. I have to find out why his boss would do something like this.

Chad picks up the phone. It's awkward, but I must find out.

"Hey, Chad, I saw the senator's press release about introducing the bill. Do you know why it was introduced without the chair?"

Chad's voice is immediately threatening.

"It would be good for folks to remember who their friends are," he says with an edge. "I think these things can go badly quickly. Things can go badly quickly. My advice to you is to stop working with your advisers. Let us who work on this deal with this stuff, without people calling in to say different things. Even if I told you to call Maria before. Don't call Maria. Don't tip the apple cart. Go silent on the Senate side."

I am astonished at the blatant attempt at controlling me. *Go silent? After his senator made a huge public display and speech for the cameras saying that they want to uplift my voice? Is this what politicians mean by being a "voice for the voiceless"? By literally gagging and intimidating victims of rape into silence so that they can get press?* My anger boils. Chad is holding millions of rape survivors' civil rights hostage all because of ego and credit. They want to pass help only once their party is in the majority, once *they* are the ones who can get political credit for it. Rape survivors' rights are beside the point.

I know exactly what to say at this moment. I have been betrayed by powerful people for so long. I have been screaming about the injustice that victims face for so long that I am out of screams. I am no longer surprised. The training from one thousand uncomfortable conversations has led me to right now.

"So you're asking me to not fight for my rights? We're flying in rape survivors who *need* these rights from different parts of the country to share their stories this month. We're already booking their tickets."

"I'm trying to help you maintain good relationships," Chad retorts. "In terms of working behind the scenes with people who are working on the bill. Don't check in with Maria. All the public stuff, that's fine—I'm talking about behind-the-scenes stuff. You just have to trust me to tell you when and where it happens. Maria's senator needs to negotiate with mine, not ask you what you and survivors care about. If she asks you, direct all her questions to us. They can't negotiate out of the room. You may get something you don't like. It's better that she negotiates with us. If she's negotiating with you, direct her to us."

"What if she calls me?"

"Of course, answer, whatever, but check in with us or else I need to treat you like any other advocate. Don't talk to anyone about this."

I'm starting to feel really anxious. "But what about my mentors? They care about me. They ask me about things other than Rise. I can't stop talking to my mentors. Sometimes we talk every week. When they ask about Rise, am I supposed to hide information from them?"

"They don't work here," Chad says, clearly losing his patience. "They are outside the building. They also don't do these things. There's a very big difference. My office is very concerned about if information we've shared comes out. If my senator hears that you talked to someone else, that's really bad. You don't want that to happen to you. And the whole thing falls apart. This whole thing can fall apart really quickly."

"What does that mean? 'Fall apart really quickly'?" I ask.

"I'm trying to prevent that from happening. That hopefully we've addressed and won't come up again. I'm trying very hard to be nice and tell you what is not helpful."

"Just to get this straight, you're holding the rights of twenty-five million rape survivors hostage because you'll have to share the credit with the other side?"

"Honey, don't take it so personally," he says coolly. "That's just how the building works."

I crawl into a fetal position on my bed. How could my pain be used as a political pawn like this? I'm reeling from another betrayal. The wool was over my eyes this whole time.

How could I have been so naive? So hopeful? How cruel it would be to be so close. I was too excited to see I was standing on a rug about to be yanked out from under me all along.

In the House of Representatives, the minority congresswoman knew the rules, and she genuinely wanted to help. So she worked across party lines for the betterment of all survivors, even stepping aside to let a majority member champion the bill so that the Speaker of the House would be more likely to bring it up for a vote. I stupidly thought that was how the Senate would go, too.

Hope is infectious, but so is panic. Steady the ship. Be the anchor. Be the lighthouse. What happens if you're the lighthouse for others, but you're also burning? What happens when you're the life raft for their rights but you're also drowning? How do I tell my team what has just happened? How do you tell a group of rape survivors fighting for their rights that our supposed champion has betrayed us? That our rights have all been snuffed out?

You do it by sobbing by yourself, alone. You hold the burden of the pain alone. Then you put on a brave face and tell the truth but keep in mind to say to each survivor that it's going to be okay. Even if you're not sure you believe it, you tell them that there's hope. Because maybe if you say it enough times, it'll come true. You tell them we will fight until the end. It's not over until it's over. Even if the statistics show a 99 percent failure rate. Even if the rules are defied.

I tell them these things, and I pray for us to win against the odds.

September 2016

The final arena of the game is the Senate floor. When a bill gets to this last stage there are several moves the final boss, the Senate Majority Leader, can take. A special move is called hotlining. This is an action that fast-tracks the bill. The way it works is that each party leader, a Democrat and Republican, emails the bill to all senators in their respective parties. The two party leaders then wait for a specified amount of time. Once that time is up, the bill can be put onto the agenda and voted on. During that specified time, any senator can anonymously place a "hold," which means they have some issues with the bill. When a senator holds a bill back longer than the duration of the time allotted, the fast-track process fails.

Maria pulls off a miracle. She convinces her senator to move the language out of the committee onto the floor by putting it up for a vote. The bill passes out of the Judiciary Committee unanimously, and now it awaits the Senate Majority Leader to put it on the agenda. Maria's boss then convinces the Majority Leader to hotline the bill for the sake of rape survivors around the country.

Chad's senator and Chad's party are also campaigning at large for women's rights. And since the bill is now endorsed by the majority party, there are no obstacles. There should be no one who places a hold on the bill. We have a straight path to victory.

We keep checking our phones every hour to see if there are any holds. Another "UNKNOWN" caller ID comes up on my phone. I hold my breath.

"There's a hold on the bill. We've checked. It's not from our side. We're clear," Maria says. "You have to figure out why Chad's party is holding it and convince them to retract it." I calmly hang up the phone. I know why Chad is holding it. Petty power over serving the people, over rape survivors who need help. I had prepared for this moment. Despite how painful it was to go through that first conversation with Chad, I had an ace up my sleeve: the law in DC is one-party-consent recording. I had recorded Chad's threats to me.

While he arrogantly tried to control me, I furiously transcribed every word he was saying. How he was holding rape survivors' rights hostage for his political ambitions. In his haughtiness and lust for power, he did not account for the fact that rape survivors need civil rights more than we need political gain. Pawns become queens when pushed to the edge of the board. We can become powerful when we're pushed far enough and have had enough.

I take the transcript and send it to the team. Our plan is for them to confront Chad's boss and offer a choice: let go of the bill and be able to take credit for it, or try to kill twenty-five million rape survivors' rights and we release the transcript. The world would know how this senator trampled over rape victims for their political gain.

Checkmate.

19.

The Gift of Grief

Still reeling from the shock, a whisper emerges from my throat, like the wind has been knocked out of my lungs: "How long have you been waiting for?"

"Since the beginning, 30. Since you arrived. I told you to sit with me. But you were too eager to run, to find a different path to save me. Come, sit with me." She looks five but now speaks with the wisdom of an eighty-year-old.

"What is the poison in you?"

"It is grief, 30, grief that has been stunted, not able to be felt, not able to pass through you. You've been grieving me all this time; you're just very good at hiding it, at numbing it, at running away from it. You've become who I needed to save me—now please become the person to save yourself."

She holds me close. The oasis begins to swell. The dunes have transformed into a salt flat desert. Water bubbles and floods the salt flat. For as far as the eye can see, the entire plain has transformed into a giant shallow lake, water no higher than a couple of inches. The water reflects the stunning sky—a giant mirror. It feels like infinity. Boundless. Just the two of us.

"How do we cure it?"

"The things that happened to you, Amanda, to me, I free you from them."

"What?"

"You've been a prisoner of your past, not thinking about it because it is painful."

The purple poison on her face has morphed into bruises of the same color. A black eye left by Dad. Red welts on her baby arms left by Mom's wooden spoon. I wince and look away. Echoes of our childhood howl in the wind.

"No! I don't want to. I can't look. I can't do it. I can't relive it." I am on my knees, sobbing with the wind.

"But it happened. No matter how much you don't want it to. I exist. This part of us exists. Look at me."

I bury my face deeper into my arms. Desperate not to look.

"You were never alone. You have me. And 15. And 22. We survived. There is an army within you. All the years you've earned that make up who you are. You are never alone. We take turns holding the perimeter."

I open my eyes. The shallow water gently ripples through a reflection of 5 and 15 and 22. 15 has the cast we had when we started Harvard. 22, a hospital band from that fateful night.

I gasp and turn to see if they are all here, but it is a mirage.

Only 5 stands. She walks over, kneels in front of me, takes my hand, and puts it on her bruised face.

"Yes, this happened to us. It's not fair, but you survived it. Look at you now. You are my dream. We can't change the things that happen to us, but the greatest power we have is to choose how we react. And you can react to change the world. We are the architect of our life, our own experience."

As she says this, the bruises, welts, and poison clear from her face.

"I am your nightmare, but it doesn't have to be that way. Choose to remember me, fully. Not as a shadowy figure, but as someone who first learned how to survive, first learned how to be strong for us so that *you* can be who *you* are today. You have peace when you make it for yourself. You have justice when you make it for yourself.

"Grief is my gift to you, Amanda. Grief is worth going through. Each stage is painful but has a lesson to teach us. Denial provides us hope. Anger gives us fuel. Bargaining teaches us value. Sadness grants us our humanity. And Acceptance . . . acceptance of grief reveals to us that we are made of love. At the end of all this, at the end of the tunnel, is healing."

The water drips steadily against the limestone of our memories. We are back in the cave where we began our journey.

5 asks, "I want to hear about you, 30. What has justice cost you?"

"Everything," I admit. "My youth, my love, my family, my dreams."

"Was it worth it?"

"Yes. Every second of it. We traded it for . . . wisdom, agency, rights, freedom, a better world for all, which is priceless. A life worth living is one that is free."

Sunlight glows through at the mouth of the entrance. I see the shadows of a brighter future flickering. The compass starts glowing.

From the other end of the cave, a dot appears larger and larger. It's 15. We run toward each other. I squeeze 15 in my arms. Reunited, we hold each other in relief and joy. The absence of 22 dawns on me.

"I didn't find her," 15 responds. "But I know where you can."

"Me?"

"Yes, you, 30. I searched for her all the way back to Bargaining's realm. He explained that the water transports you to the depths of your worst nightmare, out there in the real world."

5 chimes in gently. "Find 22's nightmare. Free her."

"I will," I promise them.

We hold on to one another. Hand in hand we take the first step, walking forward into the opening of the cave. Our steps echoing in unison. We walk toward the future, fueled by the extraordinary hope in what lies ahead. There is an end of the tunnel for all of us.

The bright sun dilates my pupils. At first the blinding light hurts my eyes. I immediately wince, my arm bracing into a defensive position to protect my sight. Deep breath. It takes a couple of seconds for me to adjust. It smells like rain just kissed the land. I hear birds chirping. There are no predators here.

Now, the warm sunlight caresses my arms. This feels new, different. I could learn to accept this.

I lower my arm. The dewdrops on the grass glisten. I feel the earth between my toes. Looking down, the most vividly colorful flowers are springing from the earth with each step I take. Periwinkle lilacs, yellow daisies, white and pink roses, teal snapdragons. Saturated. I can almost hear them laugh. Each flower, a universe. I brush my hands through them.

My hand moves to wipe away tears. I notice that I'm not holding on to my ghosts anymore. I have answered them.

I am transported from the Realm of Memory back into the real world, sitting at my desk. The invitation to my ten-year reunion at Harvard lies on my desk. I know where 22's nightmare is. I know where to find her.

20.

AMANDA'S LAW

Last night, before the vote, I went to see the stars from the steps of the Lincoln Memorial. The stars are the same ones I used to count to pass the time waiting for my mother to come and pick me up. They remind me of how far I've come.

Before the bill was put up for a vote, Maria had offered to name the law "Amanda's Law." I respectfully turned it down because I wanted this law to represent all survivors. A Survivors' Bill of Rights.

In the morning, the team and I walk with trepidation into the Senate. The bill would save my rape kit. But for most of us, we know that the criminal justice system can't give us the justice we are seeking. We only want to make sure that no one else will have to go through what we have gone through.

Our pain will have meaning. Penning our rights is the closest thing to justice we will get.

The Senate chamber has blue velvet floors dotted with mahogany desks. On its second floor, there's a balcony for guests to watch the votes. There we watch as the senators give their grand speeches. Some throw shots at each other. But ultimately the bill is put up for a vote. The gavel strikes. Unanimous passage. No more hours remain. The time loop breaks.

. . .

"I'll meet you at the restaurant. It won't be long," I say to my team as we exit the vote.

I need time to myself. It's the afternoon. The sun is setting at the Lincoln Memorial. Oddly, no one else is here. (Or no one that I can remember.) I'm by myself on the steps of greatness, where Martin Luther King Jr. had a dream, a shrine where countless others have laid their hopes and laurels. Across the reflection pond I see the US Capitol, where minutes ago Chad's senator relented. The hold was released. The nation voted unanimously to pass the bill. I convinced the nation that my rights matter. I made democracy happen by penning my own civil rights into existence.

When I think of this memory now, it is an out-of-body experience. I can see myself screaming, screaming, screaming, but really it's silent. I think if I let myself remember the sounds of this memory I'd be right back there with her, losing my mind. I can see her, Amanda at twenty-four years of age, wind sweeping across her face, flushed red, tears streaking her face, body writhing in pain. She's holding herself in her arms and finally falls, knees to the ground. All the strength she's forced herself to hold on to for so long—in case her civil rights won't pass into law, in case her justice will be slaughtered—is finally escaping out of her. That strength isn't needed anymore, like a curse breaking. This is what it looks like when the weight of history, the burden of millions of people's rights, lifts. What justice feels like.

I remember that Amanda laughing hysterically after screaming. What a feeling of peace it is, to lose your mind! Uninhibited. True. Freedom. Laugh as hard as you can, so much that you clutch your stomach because it hurts. Scream as hard as you want; rip the rage from your soul and pour it into the world. To feel it all. To feel all parts of what it means to be alive.

Insanity to one human is just reality to another. By definition, my life is insane. To challenge the US government, to take a gamble without knowing the ending. To fight a centuries-old, deeply entrenched system, thinking I could win. To quit the CIA, fingers up to the world, this twenty-something Asian girl who looks nothing like what "powerful" usually looks like.

But I think it's more insane to accept the status quo. Sanity depends on the vantage point of the viewer. Do you have a seat at the table? Or are you what's on the menu?

Life flashes before your eyes when you die. I die on these steps and am reborn.

Flash, a baby screaming after birth and my mom holding

me. *Flash*, a childhood scene of my first time riding a bicycle with my dad guiding me. To him hitting me and sobbing. *Flash*, to the thrill of opening a Harvard acceptance letter. To the despair of being in the hospital after being raped in college. *Flash*, to the stress of my CIA interrogations. To quitting the CIA process and my dreams of becoming an astronaut. *Flash*, to my first time in the halls of Congress. To now, on the steps of the Lincoln Memorial.

It's been years, a world away from the person I was when I began. I let myself feel her. Her pain. Her loneliness. Her despair. Her powerful rage. Deep breath. I close my eyes. It is over.

There's no need to fight anymore. I sit down on the marble steps. The breeze rustles the leaves. I savor my time.

Public Law 114–236
114th Congress

An Act

Oct. 7, 2016
[H.R. 5578]

To establish certain rights for sexual assault survivors, and for other purposes.

Survivors' Bill of
Rights Act of
2016.
18 USC 1 note.

Be it enacted by the Senate and House of Representatives of the United States of America in Congress assembled,

SECTION 1. SHORT TITLE.

This Act may be cited as the "Survivors' Bill of Rights Act of 2016".

SEC. 2. SEXUAL ASSAULT SURVIVORS' RIGHTS.

18 USC
3772 prec.

(a) IN GENERAL.—Part II of title 18, United States Code, is amended by adding after chapter 237 the following:

"CHAPTER 238—SEXUAL ASSAULT SURVIVORS' RIGHTS

"Sec.
"3772. Sexual assault survivors' rights.

18 USC 3772.

"§ 3772. Sexual assault survivors' rights

"(a) RIGHTS OF SEXUAL ASSAULT SURVIVORS.—In addition to those rights provided in section 3771, a sexual assault survivor has the following rights:

"(1) The right not to be prevented from, or charged for, receiving a medical forensic examination.

"(2) The right to—

Time period.

"(A) subject to paragraph (3), have a sexual assault evidence collection kit or its probative contents preserved, without charge, for the duration of the maximum applicable statute of limitations or 20 years, whichever is shorter;

"(B) be informed of any result of a sexual assault evidence collection kit, including a DNA profile match, toxicology report, or other information collected as part of a medical forensic examination, if such disclosure would not impede or compromise an ongoing investigation; and

"(C) be informed in writing of policies governing the collection and preservation of a sexual assault evidence collection kit.

"(3) The right to—

Notification.
Deadline.

"(A) upon written request, receive written notification from the appropriate official with custody not later than 60 days before the date of the intended destruction or disposal; and

"(B) upon written request, be granted further preservation of the kit or its probative contents.

"(4) The right to be informed of the rights under this subsection.

"(b) APPLICABILITY.—Subsections (b) through (f) of section 3771 shall apply to sexual assault survivors.

"(c) DEFINITION OF SEXUAL ASSAULT.—In this section, the term 'sexual assault' means any nonconsensual sexual act proscribed by Federal, tribal, or State law, including when the victim lacks capacity to consent.

"(d) FUNDING.—This section, other than paragraphs (2)(A) and (3)(B) of subsection (a), shall be carried out using funds made available under section 1402(d)(3)(A)(i) of the Victims of Crime Act of 1984 (42 U.S.C. 10601(d)(3)(A)(i)). No additional funds are authorized to be appropriated to carry out this section.".

(b) TECHNICAL AND CONFORMING AMENDMENT.—The table of chapters for part II of title 18, United States Code, is amended by adding at the end the following:

"238. Sexual assault survivors' rights .... 3772".

18 USC
3001 prec.

(c) AMENDMENT TO VICTIMS OF CRIME ACT OF 1984.—Section 1402(d)(3)(A)(i) of the Victims of Crime Act of 1984 (42 U.S.C. 10601(d)(3)(A)(i)) is amended by inserting after "section 3771" the following: "or section 3772, as it relates to direct services,".

SEC. 3. SEXUAL ASSAULT SURVIVORS' NOTIFICATION GRANTS.

The Victims of Crime Act of 1984 is amended by adding after section 1404E (42 U.S.C. 10603e) the following:

"SEC. 1404F. SEXUAL ASSAULT SURVIVORS' NOTIFICATION GRANTS.   42 USC 10603f.

"(a) IN GENERAL.—The Attorney General may make grants as provided in section 1404(c)(1)(A) to States to develop and disseminate to entities described in subsection (c)(1) of this section written notice of applicable rights and policies for sexual assault survivors.

"(b) NOTIFICATION OF RIGHTS.—Each recipient of a grant awarded under subsection (a) shall make its best effort to ensure that each entity described in subsection (c)(1) provides individuals who identify as a survivor of a sexual assault, and who consent to receiving such information, with written notice of applicable rights and policies regarding—

"(1) the right not to be charged fees for or otherwise prevented from pursuing a sexual assault evidence collection kit;

"(2) the right to have a sexual assault medical forensic examination regardless of whether the survivor reports to or cooperates with law enforcement;

"(3) the availability of a sexual assault advocate;

"(4) the availability of protective orders and policies related to their enforcement;

"(5) policies regarding the storage, preservation, and disposal of sexual assault evidence collection kits;

"(6) the process, if any, to request preservation of sexual assault evidence collection kits or the probative evidence from such kits; and

"(7) the availability of victim compensation and restitution.

"(c) DISSEMINATION OF WRITTEN NOTICE.—Each recipient of a grant awarded under subsection (a) shall—

"(1) provide the written notice described in subsection (b) to medical centers, hospitals, forensic examiners, sexual assault service providers, State and local law enforcement agencies, and any other State agency or department reasonably likely to serve sexual assault survivors; and

Public information. Web posting.

"(2) make the written notice described in subsection (b) publicly available on the Internet website of the attorney general of the State.

"(d) PROVISION TO PROMOTE COMPLIANCE.—The Attorney General may provide such technical assistance and guidance as necessary to help recipients meet the requirements of this section.

"(e) INTEGRATION OF SYSTEMS.—Any system developed and implemented under this section may be integrated with an existing case management system operated by the recipient of the grant if the system meets the requirements listed in this section.".

Establishment.

SEC. 4. WORKING GROUP.

Consultation.
42 USC
14043g–1.

(a) IN GENERAL.—The Attorney General, in consultation with the Secretary of Health and Human Services (referred to in this section as the "Secretary"), shall establish a joint working group (referred to in this section as the "Working Group") to develop, coordinate, and disseminate best practices regarding the care and treatment of sexual assault survivors and the preservation of forensic evidence.

(b) CONSULTATION WITH STAKEHOLDERS.—The Working Group shall consult with—

(1) stakeholders in law enforcement, prosecution, forensic laboratory, counseling, forensic examiner, medical facility, and medical provider communities; and

(2) representatives of not less than 3 entities with demonstrated expertise in sexual assault prevention, sexual assault advocacy, or representation of sexual assault victims, of which not less than 1 representative shall be a sexual assault victim.

(c) MEMBERSHIP.—The Working Group shall be composed of governmental or nongovernmental agency heads at the discretion of the Attorney General, in consultation with the Secretary.

(d) DUTIES.—The Working Group shall—

Recommenda-
tions.

(1) develop recommendations for improving the coordination of the dissemination and implementation of best practices and protocols regarding the care and treatment of sexual assault survivors and the preservation of evidence to hospital administrators, physicians, forensic examiners, and other medical associations and leaders in the medical community;

(2) encourage, where appropriate, the adoption and implementation of best practices and protocols regarding the care and treatment of sexual assault survivors and the preservation of evidence among hospital administrators, physicians, forensic examiners, and other medical associations and leaders in the medical community;

Recommenda-
tions.

(3) develop recommendations to promote the coordination of the dissemination and implementation of best practices regarding the care and treatment of sexual assault survivors and the preservation of evidence to State attorneys general, United States attorneys, heads of State law enforcement agencies, forensic laboratory directors and managers, and other leaders in the law enforcement community;

(4) develop and implement, where practicable, incentives to encourage the adoption or implementation of best practices regarding the care and treatment of sexual assault survivors and the preservation of evidence among State attorneys general,

United States attorneys, heads of State law enforcement agencies, forensic laboratory directors and managers, and other leaders in the law enforcement community;

(5) collect feedback from stakeholders, practitioners, and leadership throughout the Federal and State law enforcement, victim services, forensic science practitioner, and health care communities to inform development of future best practices or clinical guidelines regarding the care and treatment of sexual assault survivors; and

(6) perform other activities, such as activities relating to development, dissemination, outreach, engagement, or training associated with advancing victim-centered care for sexual assault survivors.

(e) REPORT.—Not later than 2 years after the date of enactment of this Act, the Working Group shall submit to the Attorney General, the Secretary, and Congress a report containing the findings and recommended actions of the Working Group.

Approved October 7, 2016.

LEGISLATIVE HISTORY—H.R. 5578:

HOUSE REPORTS: No. 114–707, Pt. 1 (Comm. on the Judiciary).
CONGRESSIONAL RECORD, Vol. 162 (2016):
    Sept. 6, considered and passed House.
    Sept. 28, considered and passed Senate.

EPILOGUE

In 2023, I became an astronaut with Blue Origin. When I fly, I'll become the first Vietnamese woman and the first Southeast Asian woman to break the Kármán line. When I officially was able to tell the world that I would be flying into space, Leland Melvin and Ellen Baker were my first phone calls. I include a small sign as part of the payload I'll take with me to space. Ripped from a leather notebook, in black ink, it reads, "Never Never Never Give Up."

Acknowledgments

Joy is the most radical form of rebellion. Here are the folks who keep my joy alive—the teams at AUWA Books, MCD, Farrar, Straus and Giroux, and the Wylie Agency, who believe in my story. Thank you for elevating survivor stories in a world where our voices are too often silenced. You push the culture forward to create a more equitable world.

Thank you to my friends who cried with me, laughed with me, helped me shape my writing journey over countless hours. And to the organizers who have fought in the trenches with me for survivor rights—you are the reason I find hope every morning.

As deeply as ink can convey, I am grateful to you all.

A NOTE ABOUT THE AUTHOR

Amanda Nguyen is an activist and astronaut. Nguyen ignited the Stop Asian Hate movement and passed groundbreaking legislation that protects sexual assault survivor rights in the United States and the United Nations through Rise, her civil rights accelerator. She was nominated for the 2019 Nobel Peace Prize and was named a 2022 Time Woman of the Year.